For B
— with

INSCRIBED                                    15.—

VICTOR ZARNOWITZ

UNIVERSITY OF CHICAGO

# AN APPRAISAL OF

# SHORT-TERM ECONOMIC

# FORECASTS

OCCASIONAL PAPER 104

NATIONAL BUREAU OF ECONOMIC RESEARCH

NEW YORK 1967

*Distributed by* COLUMBIA UNIVERSITY PRESS

NEW YORK AND LONDON

# RELATION OF THE DIRECTORS TO THE WORK
# AND PUBLICATIONS OF THE
# NATIONAL BUREAU OF ECONOMIC RESEARCH

1. The object of the National Bureau of Economic Research is to ascertain and to present to the public important economic facts and their interpretation in a scientific and impartial manner. The Board of Directors is charged with the responsibility of ensuring that the work of the National Bureau is carried on in strict conformity with this object.

2. To this end the Board of Directors shall appoint one or more Directors of Research.

3. The Director or Directors of Research shall submit to the members of the Board, or to its Executive Committee, for their formal adoption, all specific proposals concerning researches to be instituted.

4. No report shall be published until the Director or Directors of Research shall have submitted to the Board a summary drawing attention to the character of the data and their utilization in the report, the nature and treatment of the problems involved, the main conclusions, and such other information as in their opinion would serve to determine the suitability of the report for publication in accordance with the principles of the National Bureau.

5. A copy of any manuscript proposed for publication shall also be submitted to each member of the Board. For each manuscript to be so submitted a special committee shall be appointed by the President, or at his designation by the Executive Director, consisting of three Directors selected as nearly as may be one from each general division of the Board. The names of the special manuscript committee shall be stated to each Director when the summary and report described in paragraph (4) are sent to him. It shall be the duty of each member of the committee to read the manuscript. If each member of the special committee signifies his approval within thirty days, the manuscript may be published. If each member of the special committee has not signified his approval within thirty days of the transmittal of the report and manuscript, the Director of Research shall then notify each member of the Board, requesting approval or disapproval of publication, and thirty additional days shall be granted for this purpose. The manuscript shall then not be published unless at least a majority of the entire Board and a two-thirds majority of those members of the Board who shall have voted on the proposal within the time fixed for the receipt of votes on the publication proposed shall have approved.

6. No manuscript may be published, though approved by each member of the special committee, until forty-five days have elapsed from the transmittal of the summary and report. The interval is allowed for the receipt of any memorandum of dissent or reservation, together with a brief statement of his reasons, that any member may wish to express; and such memorandum of dissent or reservation shall be published with the manuscript if he so desires. Publication does not, however, imply that each member of the Board has read the manuscript, or that either members of the Board in general, or of the special committee, have passed upon its validity in every detail.

7. A copy of this resolution shall, unless otherwise determined by the Board, be printed in each copy of every National Bureau book.

*(Resolution adopted October 25, 1926,
as revised February 6, 1933, and February 24, 1941)*

# CONTENTS

# TABLES

# CHARTS

# ACKNOWLEDGMENTS

THIS is the first report of a study of short-term economic forecasting, supported by grants to the National Bureau from Whirlpool Corporation, General Electric Company, Ford Motor Company Fund, and U.S. Steel Corporation, as well as by other funds of the National Bureau. A grant of electronic computer time to the National Bureau by the International Business Machines Corporation was used for some of the statistical analyses in this report. This study was also supported by the Graduate School of Business of the University of Chicago through provision of ample time and excellent facilities for research. The aid of these institutions is gratefully acknowledged.

I am indebted to the National Bureau staff reading committee—Randigs Fels, Irving B. Kravis, and Ruth P. Mack—for helpful comments on an earlier version of this report. A summary of that paper was presented at the December 1964 meeting of the American Statistical Association, at which Gordon McKinley contributed valuable criticism in the discussion.

My greatest obligation is to Geoffrey H. Moore for his advice and assistance in carrying out this study and for his scrupulous reading of the manuscript. Rosanne Cole supervised the task of data processing and contributed many important suggestions and comments; this report owes much to her untiring aid.

I am grateful to Arthur F. Burns and Solomon Fabricant for their encouragement and help in planning the forecasting study in general. It is also a pleasure to acknowledge my indebtedness to Jacob Mincer, with whom I had many helpful discussions during our collaboration on a related study of methods of forecast evaluation.

I should also like to thank Nathaniel Goldfinger, Maurice W. Lee, and George B. Roberts of the National Bureau's Board of Directors for their review of the manuscript.

We owe a special debt to the many individuals and institutions who provided our forecast materials. Without their cooperation, most of the data could not have been assembled and processed.

In the course of this study, reports on some aspects of it were presented on various occasions to groups of interested economists, notably in the Econometric Workshop at the University of Chicago and at meetings in New York, Rome, Munich, and Bonn. A number of participants provided helpful comments, particularly Zvi Griliches, Wilhelm Krelle, Harry Roberts, Werner Strigel, Lester Telser, and Henri Theil.

Assistants who helped efficiently with the statistical work were Martha Callaghan Bergsten, Micaela Hickey, John Court, Dorothy Finger, and John Wiorkowski. Victor Niederhoffer contributed to the development of the sections on forecasters' consistency and related factors in Chapter 7. Marie-Christine Culbert edited the manuscript, Joan Tron improved its final version and helped in seeing it through the press, Johanna Stern aided in collecting the data, and H. Irving Forman drew the charts.

VICTOR ZARNOWITZ

# INTRODUCTION AND SUMMARY

THIS report is one of the products of the study of short-term economic forecasting, a current project of the National Bureau of Economic Research. The primary purpose of the project is to assess the accuracy of short-term forecasts of aggregate economic activity in the United States. The materials compiled and analyzed are authentic (*ex ante*) forecasts of the nation's economic fortunes for the near future—the next year or two or several shorter periods. The forecasts cover comprehensive measures of the value or volume of output for the economy as a whole and its main sectors: gross national product (GNP), its major components, and industrial production. Eventually, other variables will be added, such as personal income, employment, unemployment, and the main price indexes. The number of forecasts already collected is large and varied; when completed, the compilation should be a representative one and certainly far richer than any other such collection.

Our materials include both published and unpublished forecasts. Some of the latter were made available to the National Bureau on a confidential basis. But even for published forecasts, a decision was made at the outset of this study not to disclose the sources of the forecasts evaluated. Accordingly, none of the forecasts considered here is identified as to source. A word of explanation of this position is in order.

Forecasters draw to a large extent upon the same "raw materials," that is, on information that is widely accessible, and they variously influence one another. Few if any of them can be regarded as "independent producers," though some meet this description better than others. However, forecasters are rivals or competitors as well as co-

operators. Any statement bearing on the relative quality of a forecaster's product could be used in this competition. The National
Bureau did not undertake the present study with the intention of
supplying such information. Its purpose is scientific, and the decision
on disclosure was taken just so that purpose would remain paramount.

Economic forecasts have several aspects or dimensions, which can be
usefully measured and weighed in more than one way. Appraisals and
comparisons of forecasts may yield significantly different results depending on how this is done. A sound evaluation requires that several
measures be examined critically. It is not possible, then, to make the
procedure very simple, lest the results be incomplete and therefore
misleading. Intrinsic to the process of deriving appropriate measures
of forecasting performance are certain checks and balances which help
to make the appraisal objective and fair. But, by the same token, it
is easy to distort the appraisal, simply by quoting selectively or out of
context. In these circumstances the need to guard against possible mis-
use of the analysis is impelling. Moreover, the possibility of error in
the analysis itself cannot be entirely eliminated.

For these reasons, the sources of the forecasts reviewed are not identified. We do not believe that this reduces the scientific value of the
findings. Since we describe fully the methods of measuring forecasting
accuracy that we have used, the same methods can readily be applied
by others for purposes of comparison or verification.

The analysis of predictive accuracy yields a description of forecasting errors—their magnitude, type, and structure. The problem is to
evaluate the errors in such a way as to make meaningful inferences
about the dependability and usefulness of the forecasts.

### PLAN OF STUDY

This study is divided into eight chapters. The first gives a short description of the nature and sources of the forecasts collected. The
second presents some basic data and introduces several subjects that
are treated in detail later, such as the measurement of forecast errors
and comparisons between forecasters, forecasts, and extrapolations. It
illustrates two types of informative arrangement of the data.

Chapter 3 compares the predicted and actual changes in each successive period and reviews the correlations among them and among the
errors for different forecasters. It considers whether large errors are par-

ticularly frequent in some periods and rare in others, whether under-estimates are concentrated in some periods and overestimates in others. It discusses how the predictive errors are affected by the cyclical characteristics of the forecast period.

Chapter 4 presents the over-all record of predictive accuracy for annual forecasts of GNP, its major expenditure components, and industrial production. It shows how errors in predicting the future were affected by errors in estimating the present, to what extent errors were systematic rather than random, how often the forecasters underestimated or overestimated the actual changes, and what was the forecasters' record on turning points. It shows which of the variables presented the forecasters with particular difficulties and considers the reasons. It also discusses the effects of aggregation over the GNP expenditure sectors.

Chapter 5 examines the characteristics of multiperiod forecasts, which try to predict a sequence of values for an economic variable. It analyzes the average relations between the time span of forecasts and their accuracy, and also the implicit marginal relations. Types of error in multiperiod forecasts (under- and overestimates, directional and turning-point errors) are also discussed.

Chapter 6 presents, for the variables concerned, extrapolations of the last-known levels and changes, of average historical changes (trends), and of the estimated relations between the present and the past values of the given series. It compares macroeconomic forecasts with these mechanical extrapolations and shows the requirements of the different extrapolative models. The relation between these comparisons and the length of the time span covered by the predictions is also analyzed.

Chapter 7 compares the merits and shortcomings of certain types of forecasts. It considers the possible advantages of sectoral forecasts by experts and the effects of aggregating forecasts by individuals into an average group forecast. It examines whether meaningful comparisons can be made between the records of different forecasters, whether some have been significantly better than others. It discusses the consistency of the forecasters' record over time.

The final chapter reports briefly on the progress made thus far in other areas covered by the National Bureau's study of economic forecasting and presents an outline for further research.

I have tried to make this report as simple and nontechnical as possible, but may not have succeeded very well in that endeavor. The reason, apart from any inadequacies of exposition, is that evaluation of forecasts is a relatively complex task which can hardly be done without some statistical tools and a modicum of technical language. As a rule, however, the passages that seemed more difficult have been relegated to footnotes which need not detain the reader who is uninterested in, or unprepared for, the complications or detail involved. There are only a few sections in which the text itself contains such passages, notably that on the bias in forecasting (in Chapter 4) and those on the extrapolative models (in Chapter 6).

The reader who wishes only to acquaint himself with the main results of this study may find it sufficient to limit his attention to the "conclusions" in the next section and the following parts of the text: Chapters 1–3; Chapter 4, first three sections; Chapter 5, first section; and Chapters 7 and 8.

### CONCLUSIONS

This section lists our main findings to date. Some additional forecast data have been assembled but not yet processed, and research on some of the points mentioned is still under way. The conclusions that follow, therefore, are in part still tentative and provisional.

1. Records of forecasts of gross national product for the year ahead, covering the period between 1953 and 1963, show an average error, without regard to sign, of $10 billion. Of this, $1.8 billion is accounted for by errors in estimating the level of GNP at the time the forecast was made, and $8.2 billion by errors in predicting the changes in GNP. These errors are computed by comparing forecasts with early recorded estimates. If current, revised GNP figures are used, considerably larger errors are obtained. This is so because in most years forecasts tended to underestimate the preliminary figures, while revisions tended to raise the levels of GNP.

2. The mean absolute error of about $10 billion amounts to no more than 2 per cent of the average level of GNP in that period, but to a much larger fraction—approximately 40 per cent—of the average year-to-year change in GNP. Since the forecasting of changes is the primary objective of short-term forecasting, the latter percentage is the more significant measure of the degree of success or failure.

3. The mean absolute error of forecasts of industrial production for the same years was about 4 index points on the base 1947–49 = 100. This is about 2.7 per cent of the average level and 47 per cent of the average annual change in the production index.

4. The over-all averages conceal a considerable amount of dispersion among the average errors of different forecasters. These errors range from $7 to $14 billion for GNP forecasts between 1953 and 1963, and from 3 to 5 index points for industrial production forecasts. These figures still underestimate dispersion, inasmuch as the forecasts include some group averages which are themselves summaries of divergent individual predictions.

5. The predictions under study represent the product of several hundred forecasters. They were made by economists associated with industrial firms, banks and other financial companies, business publications, government agencies, and universities. Substantial differences between summary measures of error indicate that predictions made by individual economists or small teams for business enterprises are better than those produced by large groups or polls. This is so even though the average forecast for a group is in the long run typically more accurate than most of the forecasts of the individual members in this group because of compensating errors among the member forecasters.

6. There is also some indication that reliance on experts in particular sectors may yield better forecasts. However, it is extremely difficult to establish significant differences among the different types and sources of forecasts. The reasons are in part technical, such as the fact that forecasts for a given year are made at different dates and the late forecasts have an advantage over the earlier ones. Also, forecasts rank very differently in accuracy from one year to another.

7. Forecasts of comprehensive economic aggregates were in general more accurate in the 1953–63 period than in the early postwar period. However, there were certain special difficulties attached to the early postwar forecasts (notably the disturbances caused by World War II and later, in 1950–51, the outbreak of the Korean War and its early consequences). There is no evidence that forecasters' performance improved steadily over the period covered by the data.

8. Most forecasts underestimate the growth of the economy as measured by GNP. The underestimate is typically largest for the beginning

of a recovery from a business recession (when growth rates tend to be particularly high). Declines are less frequently underestimated than increases. Changes in series which fluctuate more and have grown less vigorously (e.g., gross private domestic investment) have been over-estimated as often as underestimated.

9. Apart from the early postwar period, few significant errors were made in end-of-year forecasts on the direction of annual changes in comprehensive economic aggregates. The timing of recent business cycle downturns was early enough to make the presence of the recession widely known by the end of the peak years (1953, 1957, 1960). This, plus the presumption that the contractions would be short, made the task of predicting annual changes relatively easy.

10. Annual forecasts of GNP and industrial production are, on the whole, more accurate than any simple extrapolation of the preceding year's level or change. Even the more refined and effective kinds of extrapolations, based on relations between present and past values of the series or on recent average rates of change, are inferior to the economists' forecasts for these variables.

11. Forecasts of GNP and the production index for one to three quarters, like the annual ones, are typically better than all types of extrapolation. However, accuracy diminishes steadily as the forecast span increases. Forecasts for four quarters or more ahead are generally not superior to extrapolations of the recent trend (measured simply by the average rate of change). The record of year-to-year forecasts does not imply any greater accuracy than this because such forecasts are generally made late in the preceding calendar year and a good record in the first two quarters will produce a moderately good record for the year as a whole.

12. Marginal errors of multiperiod forecasts do not increase system-atically, that is, average errors do not increase faster than the extension of the forecast span. In fact, decreases as well as increases in the mar-ginal errors are observed, and no strong systematic tendency emerges when an adjustment is made for the fact that the recent past and pres-ent must in part also be predicted because of the lag of information. This evidence is consistent with the idea that projection of a certain rate of growth over a sequence of short intervals has been one of the basic devices in the construction of the multiperiod forecasts.

13. The multiperiod forecasts, which include predictions for several

short intervals, are more relevant for an appraisal of turning-point errors than the annual forecasts, and they present a different picture of such errors. The results here are, on the whole, negative: the record of the numerical forecasts of GNP (like that of qualitative turning-point forecasts) does not indicate an ability to forecast the turn several months ahead. Not only were actual turns missed but also turns were predicted that did not occur. Most turning-point errors were associated with declines in the given series. This is not surprising since downturns were more difficult to predict than upturns in the postwar period.

14. Forecasts for GNP as a whole are typically much better than those for most of the component types of expenditure. This reflects in part cancellation of errors in the summation by sectors (similar to the cancellation of individual errors of opposite sign in deriving group forecasts, noted under point 5 above). Another probable reason is that some methods of forecasting, such as the use of business cycle indicators or money supply, are concerned directly with measures of aggregate economic activity rather than with any component expenditures or sectors of the economy, and hence may yield better forecasts for total GNP.

15. The errors in forecasts of percentage changes in personal consumption expenditures are much smaller than those in forecasts of gross private domestic investment. Errors in predicting government spending are of intermediate size. The greatest *need* for improvement is in forecasts of construction (particularly residential), changes in inventories, and net foreign investment. Even though these series show relatively weak trends and strong cyclical and irregular movements, and hence do not lend themselves to effective extrapolations by any simple means, their forecasts have often proved to be little better or even worse than mere extrapolations.

16. The greatest *scope* for improvement, however, probably exists in the forecasts of consumption, including those for nondurable goods and services. This is because these are smoothly growing series which would have been predicted very well in recent years by simple trend extrapolations. The average errors of consumption forecasts have typically been larger than those of such extrapolations.

17. Aggregation of short-term expectations or plans of business concerns about their outlays on plant and equipment, as developed in

periodic intentions surveys, results in better predictions of total business capital expenditures than those made independently for the entire economy. This can be inferred from comparisons between the investment forecasts in our collection which are made before and after the McGraw-Hill Survey of Investment Intentions, and also from comparisons involving the Commerce-SEC investment anticipations data.

18. Better utilization of the historical content of the series could lead to a significant improvement of the forecasts. It would seem desirable that, at some stage, trend projections should be incorporated in the forecasting process since our study shows that many forecasts looking ahead four quarters or more are inferior to simple trend extrapolations.

19. It may be possible to achieve further gains by improving the shortest forecasts. Experiments show that knowledge of the next two quarters combined with even the simplest projections for the further future would lead to annual and longer forecasts that are better than those actually on record. This suggests that forecasters may do well to concentrate primarily on the two or at most the three nearest quarters: if they improved these short forecasts (which can be much better than mere extrapolations), they would also be able to produce better longer forecasts by means of projections over the more distant periods.

20. Improvements in the record-keeping practices of forecasters are badly needed. The records should not only include the forecast but also the estimated present position (errors in the latter are, as a rule, substantial and their measurability is important). The methods used to arrive at the forecasts should be specified. Such records would facilitate future appraisals, reveal limitations of forecasts, and might suggest improvements in techniques.

# 1

## A COLLECTION OF AGGREGATIVE
## ECONOMIC FORECASTS

EIGHT sets of forecasts are used in this report; in subsequent sections they will be referred to as A, B, C, . . . H. The following is a brief summary of some of their main characteristics.

We have collected forecasts that represent a variety of sources and types. In one category are the company forecasts, which are typically the product of small professional teams made up of one or a few principal economists of a firm and a technical staff. In our collection, there are four such company forecasts from industrial, financial, and publishing fields. Another source, which supplies the largest share of the data, is forecasts by groups of business economists. There is one such group, whose membership is now about fifty, for which both summary group measures and forecasts for each individual participant were examined. This is also the case for another smaller group which includes forecasters from various industries, government, and academic institutions. Our list also includes a poll based on a very large number of forecasts (about 100 in the middle 1950's and 300 more recently), but for this set no individual forecasts are available, only medians and ranges.

The great majority of business forecasts are annual; they are made at the end of one calendar year for the next year. For a short-run analysis of business conditions and expectations, however, it is of particular interest to have forecasts for shorter and varying spans. An appraisal of turning-point forecasts, for example, can be really meaningful only for data on periods shorter than one year. Our collection includes some forecasts with spans of six, twelve, and eighteen months, some with spans of one to four quarters, and some with spans of one to six quarters. Forecasts from two sources are annual only.

Another analytical advantage of our forecasts is that some of them

are issued at relatively frequent intervals. While four of the sets
consist of forecasts made only once a year, two are forecasts made
twice a year, and one provides predictions made at quarterly intervals.
These are rich materials for the study of forecast formation and re-
vision.

Long forecast records are obviously preferable to short ones for
analytical purposes; but unfortunately they are hard to find. There is
an abundance of forecasts, mostly annual, for recent years, but very
few also cover earlier years. Few of the collected forecasts reach further
back than the early 1950's and there are none before 1947.

Each of the sets of data examined includes forecasts of GNP and
most also include the major expenditure components of GNP. An
analysis of the principal factors influencing these components, often
called the "gross national product approach," is widely used in short-
term forecasts of business activity. This approach is undoubtedly
adopted by many of the forecasters covered by this report, e.g., in
groups D and E; in some cases, it is explicitly the basis of the forecast (set B and a subset of A). However, it often represents no more
than a general framework for analysis, which leaves much scope for
the exercise of judgment. It also does not preclude the use of other
techniques, notably the indicators of cyclical turning points.

The main statistical basis of the work on indicators is a group of
series selected in National Bureau business cycle studies. Contacts
with forecasters suggest that these data are widely used, but generally
in flexible and often loose ways, as part of their statistical equipment
to help them appraise the present economic situation and outlook, not as
a mechanical predictive device. In some cases, a discussion of the indicators is included in the format of the forecast (A, C, and F).

Business forecasters, like businessmen in general, have come to de-
vote a great deal of attention in recent years to the economic role of
the government and to the relation between its policies and the business outlook. Money supply and other monetary indicators are probably important codeterminants of some of the forecasts (notably set F).

As far as one can see, very little use has been made so far of formal
econometric models in forecasts of business activity, but recently interest of business firms in this forecasting method has increased. Large
companies which have adequately staffed economic departments
familiar with computers are the most likely to use this method.

Collecting and averaging other people's forecasts can hardly be regarded as another technique of forecasting, comparable to such approaches as econometric model building or the application of selected indicators. The so-called "opinion poll" will, of course, incorporate as many different techniques as are used by the different respondents. But a set of average forecasts based on many series of individual forecasts can, nevertheless, be of substantial analytical interest. First, given a sufficiently broad basis, a composite forecast of this sort may prove useful as an indicator of expectations, in particular of the climate of opinion in the business community. Second, it can provide an interesting standard of comparison for the individual forecasts. For these reasons, we have compiled a series of averages from the available annual forecasts of GNP beginning in 1954. This set (H) includes forecasts of both individuals and groups (the latter weighted by the number of participants). Its coverage is relatively small (27–31 forecasts) in 1954–55, but much larger though very variable (77–192 forecasts) since 1956.[1]

[1] In six out of the ten years covered, the number of forecasts included exceeds 120. The main source for this compilation is the annual summary of forecasts prepared by the Federal Reserve Bank of Richmond. There is some duplication here since set H includes one of the other forecasters' groups, but it is relatively slight.

# 2

# MEASUREMENT AND PRESENTATION
# OF BASIC DATA

## ANNUAL LEVEL FORECASTS

The peak of what may be called the forecasting season is at the end of the year when predictions are made for the following calendar year. After the close of the year to which the forecasts refer, early estimates of the actual magnitudes become available; the forecasts can then be appraised by comparisons with these estimates.

Table 1 gives the results of such an appraisal for the eight sets of forecasts of GNP covering the years 1953–63. There is a column for each year which starts at the top with a figure representing the first annual estimate of GNP (line 1) reported by the Department of Commerce. Beneath that value $(A_t)$ is listed the estimated error of measurement, which is the difference between the first estimate of GNP and the current (August 1965) figure for GNP $(A_t')$. In other words, the data revisions, cumulated from the first figure published by the source up to date, are taken to measure the detectable inadequacies of observation (line 2). The errors of forecast are then presented in the form of deviations from $A_t$ of the predictions of GNP for the given year, that is, the forecast level minus "actual" level (lines 3–10).

The argument in favor of this approach is that the early estimates have probably more in common with the data inputs used by the forecaster than the subsequently revised figures. In fact, when the subsequently revised figures are used, which amounts to making the forecaster responsible for estimating the future revisions of the data, the errors tend to be considerably larger. This is readily verified in Table 1, where deviations of the predicted from the latest revised figures can be calculated for any given year simply by adding the listed errors (lines 3–10) to the revisions (line 2). Such recomputations usually result

## TABLE 1

### Eight Sets of Annual Forecasts of GNP: Individual and Average Errors and Comparisons with Simple Extrapolations, 1953-63

(billion dollars)

| | 1953 (1) | 1954 (2) | 1955 (3) | 1956 (4) | 1957 (5) | 1958 (6) | 1959 (7) | 1960 (8) | 1961 (9) | 1962 (10) | 1963 (11) | Average Error, All Years With Regard to Sign (12) | Without Regard to Sign (13) |
|---|---|---|---|---|---|---|---|---|---|---|---|---|---|
| | | | | *Actual Values of GNP and Errors of Forecasts in Each Year* | | | | | | | | | |
| | | | | | | *Actual Value and Error of First Estimate* | | | | | | | |
| 1. First estimate[a] | 367.2 | 357.2 | 387.2 | 412.4 | 434.4 | 437.7 | 479.5 | 503.2 | 521.3 | 553.9 | 585.0 | | |
| 2. Error[b] | +2.6 | −7.6 | −10.8 | −6.8 | −6.7 | −9.6 | −4.1 | +0.6 | +1.2 | −6.4 | −4.2 | −4.7 | 5.5 |
| | | | | | | *Forecast Errors[c]* | | | | | | | |
| 3. Set A | | −10.2 | −25.5 | −11.4 | −6.4 | +1.8 | −8.6 | +7.7 | −11.0 | +9.3 | −17.2 | −7.2 | 10.9 |
| 4. Set B | −7.2 | +8.8 | −17.2 | −10.4 | −4.4 | +11.3 | −4.5 | +5.8 | −7.3 | +12.1 | −18.0 | −2.8 | 9.7 |
| 5. Set C | | | | | | −2.3 | −9.1 | +8.5 | −16.3 | +12.4 | −12.3 | −3.2 | 10.2 |
| 6. Set D | | | | −8.7 | −7.0 | +1.0 | −17.0 | +8.6 | −13.5 | +0.6 | −19.2 | −6.9 | 9.4 |
| 7. Set E | −19.0 | +2.0 | −25.8 | −20.1 | −15.3 | +7.9 | −28.0 | +5.3 | −10.3 | +4.6 | −20.0 | −10.8 | 14.4 |
| 8. Set F | −6.2 | −5.2 | −16.1 | −6.4 | −6.9 | −4.4 | −4.5 | +6.8 | −12.5 | +11.1 | −9.0 | −4.8 | 8.1 |
| 9. Set G[d] | −12.0 | +5.2 | −9.6 | −6.5 | +1.0 | +4.4 | +3.3 | +10.7 | +1.8 | +12.9 | +8.4 | +1.8 | 6.9 |
| 10. Set H | | −8.7 | −22.7 | −12.2 | −5.4 | +1.1 | −16.9 | +5.6 | −9.0 | +6.3 | −15.6 | −7.8 | 10.4 |

*(continued)*

TABLE 1 (concluded)

| | Actual Values of GNP and Errors of Forecasts in Each Year | | | | | | | | | | | Average Error, All Years | |
|---|---|---|---|---|---|---|---|---|---|---|---|---|---|
| | 1953 (1) | 1954 (2) | 1955 (3) | 1956 (4) | 1957 (5) | 1958 (6) | 1959 (7) | 1960 (8) | 1961 (9) | 1962 (10) | 1963 (11) | With Regard to Sign (12) | Without Regard to Sign (13) |
| *Average Forecast Errors* | | | | | | | | | | | | | |
| 11. With regard to sign | -11.1 | -1.4 | -19.5 | -10.8 | -6.3 | +2.6 | -10.7 | +7.4 | -9.8 | +8.7 | -12.9 | -5.2[e] | |
| 12. Without regard to sign | 11.1 | 6.7 | 19.5 | 10.8 | 6.6 | 4.3 | 11.5 | 7.4 | 10.2 | 8.7 | 15.0 | | 10.0[e] |
| *Errors in Extrapolations* | | | | | | | | | | | | | |
| 13. Extrapolating level of previous year | -19.2 | +7.7 | -26.7 | -21.5 | -19.7 | +2.6 | -37.8 | -21.1 | -16.9 | -35.2 | -30.3 | -19.8 | 21.7 |
| 14. Extrapolating past average change | -3.6 | +34.2 | -14.7 | -3.5 | -3.8 | +19.3 | -23.0 | -4.3 | -0.1 | -10.1 | -11.4 | -1.9 | 11.6 |

[a]First estimates by the Department of Commerce for the preceding year, which appear in February. These figures are not comparable from year to year because of revisions.

[b]Obtained by subtracting the current (August 1965) figures for GNP from the preliminary estimates in line 1.

[c]Measured from the first estimates of GNP in line 1. The annual figures for sets A, C, D, and E were in some cases obtained by averaging forecasts for the first and second half or for the four quarters of the coming year.

[d]These forecasts are typically made in terms of base-period prices. For the purpose of these comparisons, they have been converted to current dollars, using actual prices for the forecast year. Since this eliminates the possibility of error in forecasting prices, it probably reduces the error in this set relative to the others.

[e]These figures are averages of all entries in lines 3-10, columns 1-11 (*not* averages of the entries in lines 11 and 12, which are different because the number of observations are not the same in each column).

in increased errors because the numbers added frequently agree in sign. It will be noted that in most years forecasts tended to underestimate the preliminary figure for GNP (the listed errors are negative), while revisions tended to raise the preliminary figures (most of the entries in line 2 are also negative).

Going further down the table, averages of the individual forecast errors are shown for each year, with and without regard to sign (lines 11–12). The figures at the right end of the table summarize the record of each forecast set over the entire period covered; again, averages of the forecast errors are given with and without regard to sign (columns 12 and 13).

This arrangement makes it possible to compare the forecasters' performance in and between any of the years. Reading across the table, one can see how a forecaster has done in any year and compare his individual errors with each other and with the corresponding averages. Reading down, one can compare the accuracy of different forecast sources in any year and on the average over time.[1]

In addition, the table presents the errors of two simple types of extrapolation which provide common standards for screening the forecasts. The first (line 13) consists in projecting forward the last known (or estimated) value of GNP: the level of the series the following year is assumed to be equal to that of the preceding year. The second, which is far more effective (line 14), is an extrapolation of the past average change as it could have been computed from the postwar record of GNP available up to the time the forecast was made.

These models, labeled N1 and N2* respectively, will be used extensively in this study as standards for evaluating forecasts, along with some other types of extrapolation. It should be noted here that the projections of the preceding year levels give results that are decidedly inferior to the forecasts proper, at least for the GNP series (this is not necessarily true for all other variables to be examined). The trend projections, which are based on the average changes computed from data beginning in 1947, are quite good in years of relatively moderate growth, as would be expected, but much worse in periods of booms, and very poor in recession years. As a result, they yield a small mean arithmetic error (only one of the eight forecast sets did as well in this

---

[1] Note, however, that not all of the averages in columns 12 and 13 relate to the same periods, which impairs their comparability.

respect) but a much larger mean absolute error (only one of the forecasts did worse here, although some were just a little better and the
differences may not be significant).[2]

Table 1 illustrates a simple and effective way of organizing basic
data on forecasts. Makers and users of forecasts can readily adopt such
a form to keep a running score of their own or other people's predictive successes and failures. It can suit a variety of needs because it can
be applied to forecasts of different variables for different time units
and periods, along with other types of summary measures of error and
benchmark extrapolations. To economize space I shall not introduce
such additional applications here; they will be used at later times in
the text.

### RECORDED AND PREDICTED CHANGES

A different but also informative way of presenting basic forecasting
data is illustrated in Table 2, where the changes in recorded GNP
figures are compared with the changes that were predicted. Again,
the earliest annual estimates published by the Department of Commerce serve as the basis of these comparisons, but the latest figures are
also shown (compare lines 1 and 2).

The predicted changes should be measured from the estimate of the
current position which the forecaster used as the starting point. Where
such estimates are not reported, problems arise which will be discussed
later. Three types of error can be distinguished in comparing the predicted with the actual changes: underestimation, overestimation, and
directional or turning-point errors which involve differences in sign.
Where the predicted change has the same sign as the recorded change
but is smaller (larger) than the latter, an error of underestimation
(overestimation) occurs. In Table 2, the predicted changes are marked
with different symbols to identify the under- and overestimates and
the directional errors. The symbols refer to the comparisons of predicted changes with the recorded changes according to the first estimates. The same procedure is followed for the averages, which are
taken over the forecasts from different sources in each year (line 11)
and over time for each source, with and without regard to sign (columns 12 and 13). In each case, the average predicted change is com-

---

[2] Compare the figures in columns 12 and 13 of the table.

## TABLE 2

### Eight Sets of Forecasts of Annual Changes in GNP: Individual and Average Predictions, Average Errors, and Comparisons with Simple Trend Extrapolations, 1953-63

(billion dollars)

| | 1952 -53 (1) | 1953 -54 (2) | 1954 -55 (3) | 1955 -56 (4) | 1956 -57 (5) | 1957 -58 (6) | 1958 -59 (7) | 1959 -60 (8) | 1960 -61 (9) | 1961 -62 (10) | 1962 -63 (11) | Average Predicted Changes and Errors, All Years — With Regard to Sign (12) | Without Regard to Sign (13) |
|---|---|---|---|---|---|---|---|---|---|---|---|---|---|
| **Recorded Changes[a]** | | | | | | | | | | | | | |
| 1. First estimate | 19.2 | -7.7 | 26.7 | 21.5 | 19.7 | -2.6 | 37.8 | 21.1 | 16.9 | 35.2 | 30.3 | 19.8[b] | 21.7[b] |
| 2. Latest estimate | 19.1 | .2 | 33.2 | 21.2 | 21.9 | 6.2 | 36.3 | 20.2 | 16.3 | 40.2 | 28.9 | 22.2[b] | 22.2[b] |
| **Predicted Changes[c]** | | | | | | | | | | | | | |
| 3. Set A | | -22.1§ | 5.7* | 14.0* | 17.6* | 3.9[T] | 34.8* | 32.3§ | 7.3* | 43.4§ | 14.6* | 15.2* | 19.6* |
| 4. Set B | 14.0* | -3.0* | 14.0* | 15.0* | 19.0* | 13.0[T] | 34.0* | 29.0§ | 10.0* | 46.0§ | 13.0* | 18.5* | 19.1* |
| 5. Set C | | | | | | 0.8[T] | 33.4* | 34.0§ | 2.1* | 45.3§ | 19.3* | 22.5* | 22.5* |
| 6. Set D | | | | 16.5* | 16.7* | 2.1[T] | 27.6* | 31.3§ | 3.4* | 36.0§ | 12.7* | 18.3* | 18.3* |
| 7. Set E | 4.1* | -9.9§ | 5.3* | 6.4* | 8.5* | 10.0[T] | 18.4* | 24.8§ | 3.2* | 41.7§ | 12.2* | 11.3* | 13.1* |
| 8. Set F | 15.8* | -14.0§ | 14.5* | 19.0* | 15.8* | -0.7* | 38.0§ | 31.0§ | 5.6* | 45.3§ | 22.2* | 17.5* | 20.2* |
| 9. Set G | 8.5* | -3.6§ | 19.0* | 17.3* | 21.4§ | 5.9[T] | 44.1§ | 33.5§ | 19.8§ | 46.7§ | 38.7§ | 22.8§ | 23.5§ |
| 10. Set H | -22.2§ | | 7.5* | 13.0* | 18.3* | 2.2[T] | 27.7* | 28.3§ | 7.9* | 41.7§ | 16.3* | 14.1* | 18.5* |

*(continued)*

TABLE 2 (concluded)

| | 1952 -53 (1) | 1953 -54 (2) | 1954 -55 (3) | 1955 -56 (4) | 1956 -57 (5) | 1957 -58 (6) | 1958 -59 (7) | 1959 -60 (8) | 1960 -61 (9) | 1961 -62 (10) | 1962 -63 (11) | With Regard to Sign (12) | Without Regard to Sign (13) |
|---|---|---|---|---|---|---|---|---|---|---|---|---|---|
| | | | | | Actual and Predicted Changes and Errors | | | | | | | Average Predicted Changes and Errors, All Years | |
| | | | | | Average Predicted Changes and Errors | | | | | | | | |
| 11. Average change for sets A-H | 10.6* | -12.5§ | 11.0* | 14.5* | 16.8* | 4.6ᵀ | 32.2* | 30.5§ | 7.4* | 43.3§ | 18.6* | 17.3* | 19.2* |
| 12. Average error with regard to sign | -8.6 | -4.8 | -15.7 | -7.0 | -2.9 | +7.2 | -5.6 | +9.4 | -9.5 | +8.1 | -11.7 | -3.1 | 8.2 |
| | | | | | Extrapolated Changes and Errors (N2*) | | | | | | | | |
| 13. Extrapolated change | 19.6§ | 20.7ᵀ | 15.5* | 21.7§ | 19.9§ | 20.4ᵀ | 21.6* | 18.4* | 16.8* | 25.3* | 20.5* | 20.0§ | 20.0* |
| 14. Error of extrapolation | +0.4 | +28.4 | -11.2 | +0.2 | +0.2 | +23.0 | -16.2 | -2.7 | -0.1 | -9.9 | -9.8 | +0.2ᵈ | 9.3ᵈ |

*Underestimate.

§Overestimate.

ᵀTurning-point error.

ᵃLine 1 is based on first Commerce estimates for the preceding year, which appear in February. Line 2 is based on published figures available currently (August 1965). See Table 1, lines 1 and 2 and notes.

ᵇThese figures show the changes between 1952 and 1963 (averages of entries in lines 1 and 2, columns 1-11). For comparison with forecasts A and H (1953-63), the appropriate arithmetic and absolute averages are 19.9 and 22.0; with forecasts C (1957-63), 23.1 and 24.0; and with forecasts D (1955-63), 22.5 and 23.1.

ᶜFor description of the forecast sets, see text above and Table 1, notes c and d.

ᵈAverages of the error figures in columns 1-11.

pared with the corresponding recorded change, either in the given year (columns 1–11) or for the whole period (columns 12 and 13).

The errors of the individual change forecasts can be computed by subtracting the "observed" figures (line 1) from the corresponding "predicted" figures (lines 3–10).[3] The arithmetic averages of these errors for all forecasts are listed in line 12. Compared with the corresponding average errors for the level forecasts in Table 1 (line 11), they turn out to be generally smaller. This difference, which is due to the errors in the current base estimates, will be given some attention later in this paper.

The two lines at the bottom of Table 2 refer to the change forecasts based on the trend extrapolation model N2* (see Table 1, line 14, and text above). The errors of these mechanical forecasts average out to a very small figure, less than the simple over-all average of the forecasts proper (compare the entries in lines 12 and 14 of column 12). But in some years, especially in the intervals covering the recessions of 1954 and 1958, the errors of the average change extrapolations were, understandably, very large. Taken without regard to sign, the errors of the changes predicted by means of the N2* model averaged a little higher than the errors made by forecasters.[4]

[3] Errors in terms of the revised rather than preliminary data would be obtained by using the entries in line 2 instead of those in line 1.

[4] Compare the entries in lines 12 and 14 of column 13. These are crude comparisons because they ignore the gaps in the table due to late starts or intermittent forecasting, but calculations limited to the periods actually covered by the forecasts would lead to similar conclusions or to results somewhat more favorable to the forecasters as a group.

# 3

## SHORT-RUN VARIATIONS
## IN FORECASTERS' PERFORMANCE

INCIDENCE OF FORECASTING ERRORS IN DIFFERENT PERIODS

A view often encountered in the financial and the business press is that forecasters score and err collectively—that they generally do well in some periods and go wrong in others. The reasons for the forecasters' "off years" are assumed to lie in some difficulties inherent in the type of economic change that occurred at these particular times. In other periods, when there were no such special hazards, forecasters would presumably tend to be "right."

It is also sometimes alleged that forecasts are alike because most of their authors tend to follow either a few reputed leaders or the "herd instinct." This view may well have some validity, but clearly no one has ever established just how much, since the originality of forecasts is hardly subject to reliable measurement. It certainly is true that forecasters interact in various ways. The important point here, however, is that, since all forecasters must face the vicissitudes of economic change at the same times, their products may all be similarly affected. It is, therefore, not necessary to assume that they copy from each other in order to explain why large errors may cluster in some periods and be rare in others, or why errors may be generally in one direction at one time and generally in the other direction at another.

A review of forecasters' performance in each successive year (or over shorter periods) should help to answer such pertinent questions as what the characteristics are of "good" and "bad" years for the forecasters and whether certain events surprise all forecasters in much the same way or whether they generate errors that show substantial differences in size or type.

There is little doubt that some periods present much greater obstacles to the forecaster, and hence cause larger errors, than others. In the period after World War II, the earliest years were apparently the worst in this respect. The widespread failure of predictions in these years is well known and has been ably analyzed.[1] In our materials, that failure is clearly documented. Quite generally, the forecasters represented in our sample apparently expected a major decline in economic activity to develop in 1947 and a smaller one again in 1948. Instead, large increases occurred in each of these years. As shown by the accompanying figures, the average errors of forecasts of annual percentage change for 1947–48 contrast sharply indeed with the much smaller errors for the later postwar years (per cent).[2]

|  | Gross National Product | | Industrial Production | |
|  | 1947–48 | 1949, 1954–63 | 1947–48 | 1949–63 |
|---|---|---|---|---|
| With regard to sign | −14.5 | −1.1 | −4.6 | −1.0 |
| Without regard to sign | 14.5 | 2.1 | 4.6 | 3.6 |

This was, no doubt, a grave misjudgment of the situation that few contemporary observers managed to avoid. But it is also true that the disruption of economic relationships caused by the war made the early postwar forecasts particularly vulnerable.[3]

In the forecasts of industrial production for 1950–51, very large underestimation errors were made again (particularly over the spans of twelve and eighteen months). Here the reason is, of course, obvious (*ex post facto*), namely, the outbreak of the Korean War and its early

[1] For a comprehensive appraisal, see Michael Sapir, "Review of Economic Forecasts for the Transition Period," *Studies in Income and Wealth, 11,* National Bureau of Economic Research, New York, 1949, pp. 273–367.

[2] Because of trends, the mean values of the series for the two periods differ substantially; hence it is preferable here to use errors computed by taking differences between the predicted and the actual percentage changes rather than errors based on either levels or absolute changes. However, our conclusion on the inferiority of the early postwar forecasts does not depend on which of these types of error measurement are used. Nor is it invalidated by the fact that the averages for the post-1948 period conceal some large errors of opposite sign that partly offset each other. In the data for GNP, the errors for 1947 and 1948 are larger than those in any of the subsequent years covered. In the data for industrial production, only the year 1950 produced decidedly larger errors. (It should be noted that the samples for GNP and industrial production include different forecasters and that the years 1950–53 are not covered by the GNP data.)

[3] Misspecified relationships seem to be responsible for a substantial share of errors in these forecasts. The reliance on the projected consumption function of the 1930's is a prime example (this involved underestimation of the effects of wartime accumulation of both liquid assets—the wealth factor—and pent-up demand).

consequences. As this was an exogenous event that could hardly have been foreseen, these particular errors appear largely excusable.

The period since 1953 did not witness external "shocks" of comparable magnitude, but clusters of large errors are nevertheless evident in some of these years. Table 2 shows that the increases in GNP were underestimated the most in the boom year 1955 (column 3). Consequently, the level of GNP was also underestimated the most in that year (Table 1, column 3). Errors of the same kind were also made in 1959 and 1961, which are again years of upswings following recessions, and in 1963, when the economy showed unexpected vigor after a retardation. But these movements were less vigorous than the expansion of the mid-1950's, and the underestimation errors were less (the second highest, on the average, were those made in the forecasts for 1963).

On the other hand, underestimation of the slowdown that was to result from the recession of 1957–58 caused the predicted level of GNP in 1958 to be too high. The same type of error was also common in the forecasts for 1960, which turned out to be another recession year. The retardation of 1962 was widely missed, with the result that the forecast levels were again too high. Finally, the 1954 decline, as already noted, proved to be milder than many forecasters had apparently anticipated. But all these errors connected with phases of sluggishness were much smaller than the underestimates relating to upswings or recoveries.

The results for industrial production are similar. Again, the largest errors are the underestimates for 1955. These forecasts, however, produced overestimates of levels in all years marked by either recession or retardation (including 1954) and also in 1956 and 1957. It should be recalled that the behavior of GNP and industrial production in the latter years differed considerably; the expansion of general economic activity lasted through the first half of 1957, but in the manufacturing sector it tapered off much earlier, coming to a virtual halt in 1956.

For total consumption expenditures as well as for GNP, 1955 was the year when the forecasters made their largest errors and 1963 their second largest (comparing once more the average errors of change for each year since 1953). These were all underestimates of growth, the predominant type of errors in consumption forecasts (see Table 7, line 4).

Among the forecasts of gross private domestic investment, a variable with very different properties, 1955 was again marked by the largest underestimation errors, though 1958 and 1959 were not far behind (in 1958, the large decline in the series was underestimated). Here, however, overestimates and turning-point errors were occasionally just as conspicuous; diffusion and diversity, rather than concentration in time and by type, seem to be characteristic of the errors of these forecasts (Table 7).

### YEAR-TO-YEAR COMPARISONS OF PREDICTED AND ACTUAL CHANGES

Chart 1 shows the forecasts of annual changes in gross national product for each of the eight sets A to H. In the left column, predicted changes are superimposed upon the actual ones. In the right column, the discrepancies between the two, i.e., the errors-of-change forecasts, are plotted on the same scales. The same arrangement is used in Chart 2 for the forecasts of annual changes in industrial production.

The charts make it clear that the predicted changes generally followed a course similar to that of the actual changes. This is true of both GNP and industrial production. To be sure, the correspondence is fairly close in some cases, very broad in others. It is not difficult to discern visually the more important differences among these patterns, which reflect major differences in accuracy (compare, for example, the GNP forecasts E and F). But surely the main lesson of these charts is that substantial positive correlations exist between the forecast changes and the realizations for both variables. As this implies, the time profiles of the forecasts themselves also resemble each other considerably in most cases.

The observed errors are on the whole much smaller than the corresponding changes: as already noted, the forecasts are typically better than last-level extrapolations which produce errors identical to the recorded changes. The errors, too, tend to be positively correlated for the different forecasts, consistently with the preceding comparisons. This shows itself primarily in the directional agreement between changes in the errors from one year to the next. This "co-movement" tendency in errors is indeed striking.[4]

[4] For GNP, errors of all forecasts change in the same direction in seven of the ten intervals covered; in the remaining three intervals, all but one forecast (F) show complete agreement in this respect. For industrial production, the agreement is only slightly less pronounced.

# CHART 1

## Eight Sets of Annual Forecasts of GNP, Actual and Predicted Changes and Errors, 1953–63

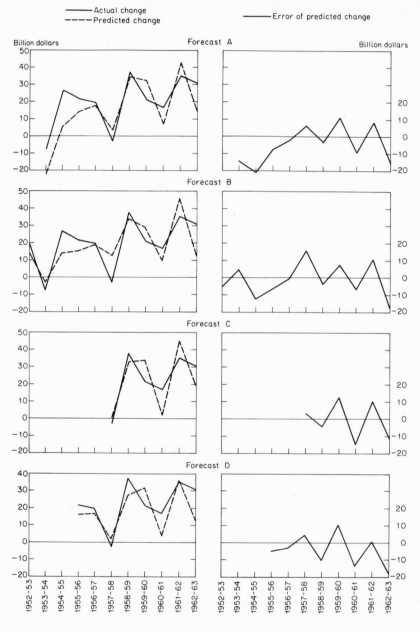

## CHART 1 (concluded)

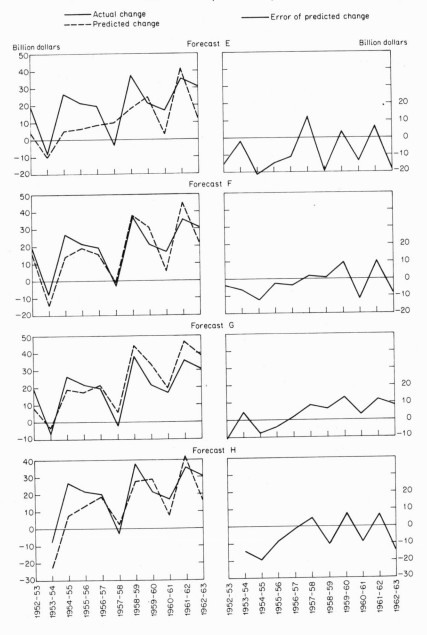

## CHART 2

*Seven Sets of Annual Forecasts of Industrial Production, Actual and Predicted Changes and Errors, 1953–63*

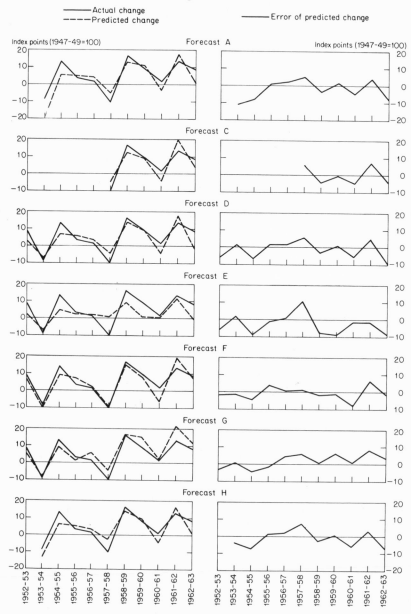

Finally, a comparison of Charts 1 and 2 discloses some significant similarities between the forecast and error patterns for GNP and industrial production. These reflect the correlation between the actual year-to-year changes in the two variables.

### FORECASTING AND BUSINESS CYCLES

The year-to-year comparisons discussed with the aid of Charts 1 and 2 suggest that predictive errors are affected by the cyclical characteristics of the forecast period. Table 3, which uses forecasts for quarters and half-years, demonstrates this still more clearly. The levels of GNP and industrial production are underestimated the most in the first year of expansion, when the increases in these series are very large. Later in the expansion, when the increases are usually smaller, the levels are underestimated much less and may even be overestimated, as happened in the unexpected retardation of 1962 (see Table 3, line 5). In contractions, overestimation of the levels is the rule, sometimes because the downturn is missed and sometimes because the decline turns out to be larger than predicted.[5]

These cyclical differences among errors can be observed in forecasts of different spans. For each of these stages—early recovery, later expansion, contraction—there are signs of the familiar characteristic of errors to increase with the forecast span. For the longest forecasts included, the eighteen-month predictions of group D, the errors are about equally large in the early and in the late expansion, and the interstage differences are not significant statistically. Elsewhere, however, such differences are definitely significant according to the analysis of variance.[6]

[5] Opposite cases, in which the decline was smaller than expected and as a result the level was underestimated, also occurred (notably in the 1954 recession, as observed earlier for the annual forecasts). These errors, however, are outweighed in most of the contraction averages by the more frequent errors of the types referred to in the text.

[6] The results of that analysis are summarized below. The computed $F$-values are the ratios of the greater to the lesser estimate of variance, in this case, of the variance of error between cycle phases to the variance of error within cycle phases.

|  | GNP Forecasts (all spans) | | Indus. Product. Forecasts (D) | | |
|---|---|---|---|---|---|
|  | A | C | 6 mos. | 12 mos. | 18 mos. |
| Computed $F$-ratio | 6.4 | 28.9 | 10.4 | 5.0 | 1.6 |
| 5 per cent level of $F$-ratio | 3.7 | 3.2 | 3.3 | 3.3 | 3.7 |

TABLE 3

*Selected Forecasts of GNP and Industrial Production: Mean Errors*
*Classified by Span and Cyclical Characteristics of the*
*Forecast Period, 1947-62*

| Line | Forecast Set, Period Covered, and Stage[a] | Span of Forecast (months) | | | | | | All Spans (7) |
|---|---|---|---|---|---|---|---|---|
| | | Three (1) | Six (2) | Nine (3) | Twelve (4) | Fifteen (5) | Eighteen (6) | |
| | | *Mean Errors of GNP Forecasts*[b] *(billion dollars)* | | | | | | |
| | Set A, 1949, 1955-63[c] | | | | | | | |
| 1. | Recovery | | −18.2 | | −20.2 | | | −19.2 |
| 2. | Upswing | | −3.5 | | −5.6 | | | −4.4 |
| 3. | Contraction | | −0.9 | | +2.8 | | | +1.0 |
| | Set C, 1958-62[d] | | | | | | | |
| 4. | Recovery | −6.6 | −11.7 | −14.7 | −20.3 | −32.6 | | −14.0 |
| 5. | Upswing | +1.5 | +3.7 | +3.4 | +3.6 | +1.2 | | +2.9 |
| 6. | Contraction | +0.1 | +4.7 | +8.9 | +9.2 | +9.6 | | +4.6 |
| | | *Mean Errors of Industrial Production Forecasts*[e] *(1947-49 = 100)* | | | | | | |
| | Set D, 1947-62[f] | | | | | | | |
| 7. | Recovery | | −5.7 | | −6.9 | | −10.4 | −7.1 |
| 8. | Upswing | | −1.2 | | −4.8 | | −10.3 | −4.4 |
| 9. | Contraction | | +3.6 | | +4.8 | | −0.4 | +3.2 |

[a]The following terms are used for brevity: recovery = the first year of expansion; upswing = the rest of expansion. The classification attempts to approximate as closely as possible the NBER business cycle chronology.

[b]Errors of level forecasts.

[c]Based on forecasts for the first and second half of the coming year.

[d]Based on forecasts made quarterly for sequences of four quarters ahead.

[e]Errors of level forecasts. The forecasts for the span in column 6 cover the period from 1948 through the first half of 1956.

[f]Based on forecasts made twice in the year for two or three semiannual periods ahead.

To understand how such results might occur, let us distinguish two predictive patterns, both of which would underestimate current cyclical changes, though in very different ways. First, imagine a series of forecasts which reproduces well, but with a short lag, the fluctuations in the actual series. The observed cyclical amplitudes need not be underestimated but the current changes at certain stages of the cycle will be. Second, imagine a series of forecasts which reproduces well the trend, but not the cyclical movements, of the actual values. The predictions simply cut across the fluctuations, so that both the cyclical amplitudes and the current short-period changes are underestimated.

Some forecasts resemble more the lagging cyclical model, others the trend-projection model. In Chart 3, the former is illustrated by forecast C and the latter by forecast G, for GNP during 1958–61. Both these sets consist of forecasts made for several quarters ahead, which in the chart are linked together into chains that fan out to the right from points representing the forecasters' estimates of the current position. The forecasts are made twice or four times in a year, hence the chains overlap. The C chains have "kinks" in 1958 and 1960–61, which lag behind the turning points in GNP; the G chains show no kinks at all.

Forecasts of the trend-projection type may come out rather well in measures of average error if they have no large bias, that is, if they neither underestimate nor overestimate the trend substantially.[7] It is clear, however, that such forecasts must be regarded as failures as far as recognition of turning points is concerned. The chain forecasts with cyclical patterns can be more useful in this role, even when they are late.

[7] The quarterly chain forecasts G for 1955–63 do show a significant overestimation bias for both GNP and industrial production (see Tables 9 and 10 and accompanying text). Incidentally, the annual forecasts G show little over-all bias merely because their underestimation errors in earlier years, 1953–57, largely offset the later overestimates (see Tables 1 and 2).

## CHART 3

*Two Sets of Chain Forecasts of GNP and the Corresponding
Actual Values, 1957–62*

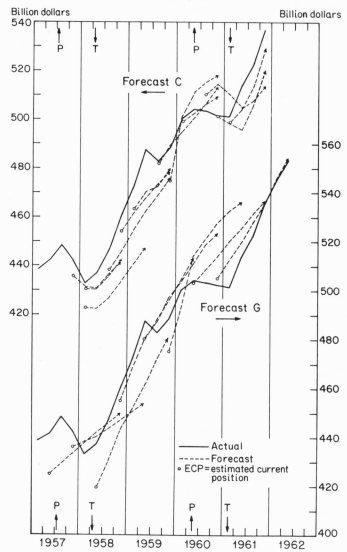

NOTE: P and T represent business cycle peaks and troughs.

# 4

# SUMMARY MEASURES AND TYPES
# OF ERROR

AVERAGE ERRORS OF ANNUAL FORECASTS
OF GNP AND INDUSTRIAL PRODUCTION

The over-all averages in Tables 1 and 2 indicate that the errors in the annual forecasts of gross national product averaged about $9 to $10 billion disregarding sign. They appear small—about 2 per cent—compared with the average level of GNP, but they are big enough to make the difference between a good and a bad business year. The average year-to-year change in GNP over 1953–63 amounted to approximately $22 billion. Thus the errors were, in terms of absolute averages, not quite one-half the size of the errors that would have been produced by assuming that next year's GNP would be the same as last year's.

On the other hand, it is important to realize that aggregates as comprehensive and complex as GNP are beset by conceptual and estimation difficulties that make their measurement quite difficult and imprecise. When the series to be predicted is subject to substantial errors of observation, forecasting becomes particularly hazardous. A mean forecasting error of $10.0 billion does not appear very large relative to a mean of $5.5 billion in the revisions of the given series (see the absolute averages in Table 1, column 13).

In the index of industrial production, short-term fluctuations play a greater role and trend a lesser one than in GNP, which should make forecasting the index more difficult. On the other hand, revisions are much less disturbing for industrial production than for GNP. The relation between the forecasting errors and the variability of the data is not very different for the two series. The average errors of the annual forecasts of industrial production varied in the narrow range of 4 to 5 index points (1947–49 = 100). This compares with year-to-year changes averaging about 8 to 10 index points, as shown in Table 4 (columns 1 and 2, lines 16–22).

Table 4 collects all the salient statistics for an evaluation of the average performance of both GNP and industrial production forecasts in recent years. In order to facilitate comparisons, the measures for GNP are computed not only in billion dollars but also in index numbers (1947–49 = 100) to make them dimensionally similar to the figures for the industrial production index. Comparisons for the same sources and periods suggest that in most cases predicted changes in industrial production were somewhat larger than those in GNP, even though the actual changes were somewhat smaller in the former series (see columns 1 and 2, lines 9–22). The absolute errors tend to be larger for the industrial production forecasts (columns 3 and 4).

However, comparisons of this sort are difficult and necessarily crude when limited to absolute error measures. The main impression one gets here, for example, is that the changes and errors are quite similar for the two variables when expressed in index numbers with a common base. This is clearly insufficient, though interesting; it is necessary to move beyond such impressions, and to this end measures of relative forecast accuracy will be needed.

Measuring the errors relative to the level of the series, however, is not a satisfactory solution. Thus, a typical error of 2 per cent may be viewed as small for a series whose variations average 10 per cent, but it must be judged large indeed for a series whose variations average 1 per cent. To anticipate a theme developed later in this study, measures of relative accuracy should take into account the properties of the predicted variables which make for differences in the degree of difficulty that confronts the forecaster. An attempt to develop such measures will involve comparisons of forecasts with types of extrapolation. Meanwhile, there is still much to be learned from the absolute accuracy measures now under consideration.

### ERRORS OF LEVELS, CHANGES, AND BASE VALUES

The simplest measure of error is obtained by comparing the predicted and the actual *levels,* but it is perhaps more important to compare predicted and actual *changes.* The error in the change will be the same as that in the level when the actual level at the time of the forecast is known. As a rule, however, it is not known, and the two will differ

TABLE 4

Annual Forecasts of GNP and Industrial Production: Average Actual and Predicted Changes and
Average Errors of Forecasts of Levels, Changes, and Base Values, 1951-63

| Line | Forecast Set[a] | Period Covered | Mean Absolute Changes | | Mean Absolute Error, $|\overline{E}|$ | | | Mean Error, $\overline{E}$ | | |
|---|---|---|---|---|---|---|---|---|---|---|
| | | | Actual[b] (1) | Predicted (2) | Level (3) | Change (4) | ECP[c] (5) | Level (6) | Change (7) | ECP[c] (8) |
| | | | *Gross National Product (billion dollars)* | | | | | | | |
| 1. | A | 1954-63 | 22.0 | 19.6 | 10.9 | 9.9 | 3.5 | -7.2 | -4.7 | -2.4 |
| 2. | B | 1953-63 | 21.7 | 19.1 | 9.7 | 8.4 | 2.5 | -2.8 | -1.3 | -1.5 |
| 3. | C | 1958-63 | 24.0 | 22.5 | 10.2 | 9.4 | 3.3 | -3.2 | -0.6 | -2.6 |
| 4. | D | 1956-63 | 23.1 | 18.3 | 9.4 | 8.1 | 2.7 | -6.9 | -4.2 | -2.7 |
| 5. | E | 1953-63 | 21.7 | 13.1 | 14.4 | 12.6 | 4.0 | -10.8 | -8.5 | -2.3 |
| 6. | F | 1953-63 | 21.7 | 20.2 | 8.1 | 6.3 | 2.9 | -4.8 | -2.3 | -2.5 |
| 7. | G | 1953-63 | 21.7 | 23.5 | 6.9 | 7.1 | 1.7 | 1.8 | 3.0 | -1.2 |
| 8. | H | 1954-63 | 22.0 | 18.5 | 10.4 | 9.5 | 3.1 | -7.8 | -5.8 | -1.9 |
| | | | *Gross National Product (1947-49 = 100)* | | | | | | | |
| 9. | A | 1954-63 | 8.9 | 7.9 | 4.4 | 4.0 | 1.4 | -2.9 | -1.9 | -1.0 |
| 10. | C | 1958-63 | 9.7 | 9.1 | 4.1 | 3.8 | 1.3 | -1.3 | -0.3 | -1.0 |
| 11. | D | 1956-63 | 9.4 | 7.4 | 3.8 | 3.3 | 1.1 | -2.8 | -1.8 | -1.1 |
| 12. | E | 1953-63 | 8.8 | 5.4 | 5.8 | 5.0 | 1.6 | -4.4 | -3.4 | -0.9 |
| 13. | F | 1953-63 | 8.8 | 8.2 | 3.3 | 2.6 | 1.2 | -2.0 | -1.0 | -1.0 |
| 14. | G | 1953-63 | 8.8 | 9.5 | 2.8 | 2.9 | 0.7 | 0.7 | 1.2 | -0.5 |
| 15. | H | 1954-63 | 8.9 | 7.5 | 4.2 | 3.8 | 1.2 | -3.2 | -2.4 | -0.8 |

(continued)

TABLE 4 (concluded)

| Line | Forecast Set[a] | Period Covered | Mean Absolute Changes | | Mean Absolute Error, \|E\| | | | Mean Error, Ē | | |
|---|---|---|---|---|---|---|---|---|---|---|
| | | | Actual[b] (1) | Predicted (2) | Level (3) | Change (4) | ECP[c] (5) | Level (6) | Change (7) | ECP[c] (8) |
| | | | *Industrial Production (1947-49=100)* | | | | | | | |
| 16. | A | 1954-63 | 8.6 | 8.4 | 4.8 | 5.0 | 0.6 | -2.2 | -2.0 | -0.2 |
| 17. | C | 1958-63 | 9.8 | 8.8 | 4.6 | 4.4 | 0.5 | -0.3 | -0.3 | 0.02 |
| 18. | D | 1954-63[d] | 8.6 | 7.2 | 4.5 | 4.1 | 1.0 | -0.6 | -1.0 | 0.4 |
| 19. | E | 1951-63[d] | 8.1 | 4.0 | 4.5 | 4.9 | 2.4 | -0.4 | -2.3 | 1.9 |
| 20. | F | 1953-63 | 8.6 | 9.1 | 3.9 | 2.8 | 1.8 | 0.8 | -0.7 | 1.5 |
| 21. | G | 1953-63 | 8.6 | 9.3 | 4.2 | 3.6 | 0.9 | 2.5 | 1.9 | 0.6 |
| 22. | H | 1954-63 | 8.6 | 7.6 | 3.8 | 4.1 | 1.0 | -0.8 | -1.1 | 0.4 |

[a]For a brief description of the forecasts, see Chapter 2 and Table 1, notes c and d.

[b]First estimates by the Department of Commerce (see Table 1, note a).

[c]Estimated current position, or base of the forecast. The base values are forecasters' own estimates for sets A (since 1957), B, C, F, and G. For the other sets, they are computed as follows: A (before 1957) — weighted averages of the last known position and the last reported relative change; D and H — sum of the last known level and the average annual change of the series up to the time of the forecast (N2* projection); E — weighted average of the last known level and the projection just described.

[d]Figures for industrial production forecasts covering periods comparable to GNP forecasts are:

| | | (1) | (2) | (3) | (4) | (5) | (6) | (7) | (8) |
|---|---|---|---|---|---|---|---|---|---|
| D | 1956-63 | 7.4 | 8.0 | 3.9 | 4.0 | 0.6 | -0.4 | -0.5 | +0.1 |
| E | 1953-63 | 3.7 | 8.6 | 4.8 | 5.0 | 2.5 | -0.8 | -2.8 | +2.0 |

by the amount of error in the estimated current position or base of the forecast.[1]

Regrettably, the estimated current position (ECP) is not always reported by the forecasters. Where such base estimates are not given they must be imputed, if the change forecasts are to be analyzed. Our imputations are based on extrapolative methods; where reported ECP's are given in some years but not in others, the estimates for the latter also utilize the information for the former.[2] The imputations cannot be shown to be "wrong" (or "right") but undoubtedly have shortcomings. All that can be claimed is that they seem on the whole reasonable when compared with the reported ECP's.

The ECP errors are, of course, typically smaller than the errors in the forecasts proper. One would expect the present or the recent past to be better known than the future. Looking at the mean absolute errors in Table 4, one finds no exceptions to this rule (compare columns 3 and 5). However, the ECP errors are by no means negligible. They average about one-fourth or one-third of the corresponding errors of the level forecasts for GNP, and from an eighth to more than half for industrial production.

The error of each level forecast is the algebraic sum of the ECP error and the error of the predicted change (see footnote 1). For the GNP forecasts, errors of base have on the average the same (negative) signs as the larger errors of the future levels (Table 4, columns 6 and 8). Accordingly, the errors of change tend to be less than the errors of level (compare columns 3–4 and 6–7).[3] For industrial production, errors of base and of level often differ in sign, and there is less regularity in the relation between the level and the change forecasts (Table 4, lines 16–22).

[1] Let the level error be defined as $E_{t+1} = P_{t+1} - A_{t+1}$, where $P$, $A$, and $E$ denote the prediction, the actual value, and the error, respectively; $t$ is the current and $(t+1)$ the next year. The predicted change is $P_{\Delta(t+1)} = P_{t+1} - A_t{}^*$ where $A_t{}^*$ is a preliminary estimate of the current position (ECP). The error of the change forecast is $E_{\Delta(t+1)} = P_{\Delta(t+1)} - \Delta A_{t+1}$, where $\Delta A_{t+1} = A_{t+1} - A_t$. The error of ECP is $E_t = A_t{}^* - A_t$.

It follows directly from these definitions that

$$E_{\Delta(t+1)} = P_{t+1} - A_t{}^* - (A_{t+1} - A_t) = E_{t+1} = E_t.$$

Hence, if $A_t{}^* = A_t$ (the ECP error is zero), then $E_{\Delta(t+1)} = P_{t+1} - A_{t+1} = E_{t+1}$.

[2] For brief descriptions of how the ECP's were computed, see Table 3, note c.

[3] The errors of the annual level forecasts for GNP average $10 billion when taken without regard to sign; the errors of the corresponding change forecasts average slightly more than $8 billion, or 18 per cent less (see Tables 1 and 2, line 12, col. 13).

FORECASTS OF MAJOR EXPENDITURE COMPONENTS OF GNP

Forecasts of GNP are frequently built upon forecasts of GNP components, which are first derived separately and then combined, with varying amounts of attention given to their interdependence and consistency. Forecasts of total GNP may benefit from a partial cancellation of errors in forecasts of the components. This is definitely preferable to the opposite case of positively correlated and mutually reinforcing errors, which would make the predictions of GNP worse than those of its components and possibly invalidate them altogether. But gross inaccuracies in the component forecasts are, of course, always disturbing, even if these errors happen to be largely compensating. In extreme cases of this sort, the comprehensive aggregate forecast could be regarded as "good for the wrong reasons."

On the other hand, some methods of forecasting are concerned directly with measures of aggregate economic activity such as GNP, rather than with any GNP components or sectors of the economy. Forecasts using money supply, for example, fall into this category, as do indeed forecasts based on composite evaluation of business cycle indicators. These methods, therefore, may well yield better forecasts for GNP than for the components, which is quite understandable.

Annual forecasts of the major expenditure components of GNP have been analyzed for the following periods and sets: 1953–63, B and F; 1958–63, A and C.[4] Table 5 summarizes the results. It is based on errors computed by taking differences between the predicted and the actual percentage changes. The dollar levels of the GNP components differ drastically; the use of percentage changes enables us to make some comparisons between these variables that could not sensibly be made in terms of dollar changes.[5]

Looking at the summary measures in Table 5, column 1, one finds

[4] Forecasts A refer to the last quarter of the next year (at annual rates), not to the total for the year (except for 1958). They have therefore longer spans than the other forecasts which are all annual, and are not to be compared with the latter (forecasts with longer spans tend to have larger errors, see Chapter 5). This obviously does not affect the comparisons between forecasts for different variables (from any given source), which are the main concern of the present analysis.

[5] Using the symbols introduced earlier (see footnote 1), the error in predicting percentage change in a series from the base period $t$ over the span $i$ is defined as

$$\left( \frac{P_{\Delta(t+i)}}{A_t^*} - \frac{\Delta A_{t+i}}{A_t} \right) \cdot 100, \text{ where * denotes a preliminary estimate.}$$

# TABLE 5

*Forecasts of Relative Changes in Major Components of GNP:*
*Summary Measures of Error, 1953-63*

(percentage points)

| Line | Predicted Variable | Mean Absolute Error[a] $\overline{|E|}$ (1) | Mean Error[a] $\overline{E}$ (2) |
|------|-------------------|------------------|------------|
| | *Forecast Set B: 1953-63* | | |
| 1. | Gross national product | 1.88 | −0.31 |
| 2. | Personal consumption expenditures | 1.25 | −0.16 |
| 3. | Gross private domestic investment | 11.69 | −2.23 |
| 4. | Plant and equipment | 6.42 | −3.51 |
| 5. | Housing | 10.95 | −6.83 |
| 6. | Total government expenditures | 1.99 | +0.81 |
| 7. | Federal | 4.29 | +0.91 |
| 8. | State and local | 1.46 | −1.24 |
| | *Forecast Set F: 1953-63* | | |
| 9. | Gross national product | 1.44 | −0.60 |
| 10. | Personal consumption expenditures | 1.51 | −0.70 |
| 11. | Gross private domestic investment | 6.20 | −1.42 |
| 12. | Total government expenditures | 1.19 | +0.42 |
| | *Forecast Set F: Other Periods*[b] | | |
| 13. | Consumer durables | 4.44 | +2.09 |
| 14. | Consumer nondurables | 1.24 | +0.92 |
| 15. | Consumer services | 1.64 | −0.88 |
| 16. | Producers' durables | 5.01 | −1.79 |
| 17. | Nonresidential construction | 3.00 | −1.02 |
| 18. | Residential nonfarm construction | 7.00 | −3.83 |
| 19. | Federal government expenditures | 1.37 | +0.10 |
| 20. | State and local expenditures | 1.05 | −0.76 |
| | *Forecast Set A: 1958-63*[c] | | |
| 21. | Gross national product | 1.79 | +0.02 |
| 22. | Personal consumption expenditures | 0.92 | +0.05 |
| 23. | Consumer durables | 4.57 | +0.67 |
| 24. | Gross private domestic investment | 9.08 | +2.45 |
| 25. | Producers' durables | 5.50 | −2.70 |
| 26. | New construction | 3.85 | −3.78 |
| 27. | Total government expenditures | 2.73 | −0.83 |

*(continued)*

TABLE 5 *(concluded)*

| Line | Predicted Variable | Mean Absolute Error[a] $\overline{\lvert E \rvert}$ (1) | Mean Error[a] $\overline{E}$ (2) |
|------|--------------------|--------------------|------------|
| | *Forecast Set C: 1958-63* | | |
| 28. | Gross national product | 1.87 | −0.07 |
| 29. | Personal consumption expenditures | 1.36 | −0.25 |
| 30. | Gross private domestic investment | 8.03 | +1.83 |
| 31. | Plant and equipment | 4.72 | +0.11 |
| 32. | Residential construction | 6.97 | −1.90 |
| 33. | Total government expenditures | 1.44 | −1.04 |
| 34. | Federal | 2.92 | −0.89 |
| 35. | State and local | 1.90 | −1.90 |

[a]Based on errors of percentage change as defined in text and footnote 5.

[b]Entries on lines 13-15 refer to 1959-63; lines 16, 19, and 20, to 1955-63; lines 17 and 18, to 1956-63.

[c]Refer to the last quarter of the next year (at annual rates), not to the total for the year (except for 1958, which is an annual forecast). See note 4.

that the errors in predicting percentage changes in personal consumption are far smaller than those in forecasts of gross private domestic investment (GPDI). The errors for total government spending are moderate: larger than those in consumption but much smaller than those in investment.

Within aggregate consumption, the errors are much larger for durable goods than for either nondurables or services. Within aggregate investment, the errors for housing or residential construction are particularly large: they exceed the errors for plant and equipment (in sets B and C) and the errors in both producers' durables and nonresidential construction (in set F). A different breakdown shows the record for producers' durable equipment to be worse than that for total new construction (in set A).[6]

[6] Taken together, these results suggest that forecasts of nonresidential construction must be considerably better than those of producers' durables, offsetting the very large housing errors. This is actually so in set F for which a construction breakdown is available (see lines 16–18 in the table).

These results agree with what would be generally expected. Spending for nondurables and services is dominated by stable growth tendencies, which lend a measure of stability to over-all consumption, while outlays for consumer durables are much more volatile. Investment is, needless to say, much more volatile than consumption. Expenditures on producers' durables have been less stable than construction in recent times. The more volatile a series, the more difficult is the prediction of its relative changes and the greater the probable forecast error.

Expenditures on housing have been restrained during business expansions by a scarcity of mortgage credit and stimulated during recessions by greater availability of credit. These countercyclical effects cause spending on residential construction to behave quite differently from other major expenditure categories. Failure to recognize such differences may be largely responsible for the particularly bad showing of the housing forecasts.

The errors in percentage change forecasts for total GNP are, on the average, much smaller than those for most of the component types of expenditures. Thus, only consumption and, in some forecasts, total government or state and local expenditures were predicted as well as, or better than, total GNP (Table 5, column 1). This indicates that the aggregation by sectors has, in fact, been associated with a very substantial cancellation of errors.

Measures of relative change errors need to be supplemented by measures in dollar terms for two reasons. First, the mean arithmetic errors of the sectoral forecasts add up to the average error for total GNP, enabling us to observe the extent to which errors for the different types of expenditure either cumulate or offset each other and also to compare the corresponding averages without regard to the signs of the errors. Second, the components of GNP that become negative—net change in inventories and net foreign investment—can be analyzed only in absolute, not in relative, terms.

Table 6 summarizes the errors of absolute changes for the two main sources of sectoral forecasts in our annual data—sets B and F. The means of these errors, like those in Table 5, column 2, are predominantly negative (columns 2 and 4), which is typical for predictions of changes in total GNP as well as industrial production (see Table 4, col. 7). Only government expenditures and net changes in inventories

TABLE 6

*Summary Measures of Error in Two Sets of Forecasts of Absolute
Changes in Major Components of GNP and Investment, 1953-63*

(billion dollars)

|  |  | Forecast Set B | | Forecast Set F | |
|---|---|---|---|---|---|
| Line | Component of GNP or Investment | Mean Absolute Error, $\lvert E \rvert$ (1) | Mean Error, $E$ (2) | Mean Absolute Error, $\lvert E \rvert$ (3) | Mean Error, $E$ (4) |
| 1. | Plant and equipment | 2.64 | −1.29 | | |
| 2. | Producers' durables | | | 1.21[a] | −0.41[a] |
| 3. | Residential construction | 1.59 | −0.92 | 1.29[b] | −0.79[b] |
| 4. | Nonresidential construction | | | .56[b] | −0.19[b] |
| 5. | Net change in inventories | 2.75 | +0.76 | 2.16[c] | +1.10[c] |
| 6. | Gross private domestic investment | 5.86 | −1.43[d] | 3.87 | −0.60 |
| 7. | Personal consumption expenditures | 3.79 | −0.41 | 4.16 | −1.67 |
| 8. | Government expenditures | 1.76 | +0.80 | 1.06 | +0.33 |
| 9. | Net foreign investment | 1.35 | −0.29 | 1.36 | −0.37 |
| 10. | Gross national product | 8.37 | −1.28[e] | 6.34 | −2.33[e] |

[a] For 1955-63.

[b] For 1956-63.

[c] For 1954-63.

[d] Sum of lines 1, 3, and 5 does not add to total in line 6 because of rounding.

[e] Sum of lines 6-9 does not add to total in line 10 because of rounding.

have positive mean errors in both sets. The averages for the component
figures are, in general, smaller absolutely than the corresponding figures for GNP (the investment forecasts in set B provide an exception).
They conceal a greal deal of variation in sign among the errors, as
witnessed by the large differences in absolute size between the paired
entries in columns 1–2 and 3–4 (this cancellation of errors is particularly pronounced in forecasts of set B).

## BIAS IN FORECASTING

A set of forecasts is said to contain a bias if it typically understates
or overstates the corresponding actual values. Thus, the criterion of

the absence of bias would be that in the "long run" (that is, for sufficiently large numbers of comparable forecasts), predictions and realizations should be on the average equal.[7] Actually, strict equality of the averages cannot be expected in the limited samples that can be observed, and the criterion is to be understood to mean that for unbiased forecasts the difference between the averages is not significant in the statistical sense.

To give some examples of biased forecasts, consider a fluctuating series which rises in good times and falls in bad ones. A strong pessimistic bias would be illustrated by forecasts that consistently specified lower levels than those observed for that series, which implies predictions of too small increases and too large decreases. A strong optimistic bias is the reverse: forecasts of higher than the actual levels, that is, of too large increases and too small decreases.

A simple measure of bias is the mean error, i.e., the difference between the means of actual and predicted values. Each observed error can thus be thought to consist of a bias, which is the average error over the entire period, and the deviation of the observed error from the average. The bias, therefore, is the constant element in the errors, since it is the same for each observed error, while the remainder reflects the variation among the recorded errors measured from this average.

A measure of the over-all accuracy of forecasts, which can be conveniently used to separate the bias from the remaining error, is the mean square error $M_P^2$, computed by squaring the individual forecast errors and averaging the results. The mean square error is the sum of two components: the square of the mean error (or bias), and the variance of the errors.[8]

The mean square error analysis involves more technical apparatus and language than I wish to use in this paper; the interested reader may consult another report in the National Bureau project on forecasting for a further discussion of the statistical concepts just outlined

[7] This is just a translation into a less technical language of the standard statistical definition of bias as the inequality of "expected values."

[8] For $n$ time periods ($t$),

$$M_P^2 = \frac{1}{n} \sum_{t}^{n} (P_t - A_t)^2 = \bar{E}^2 + S_E^2,$$

where $\bar{E}^2 = (\bar{P} - \bar{A})^2$ is the squared mean error and $S_E^2$ is the variance of errors. In the absence of bias, $\bar{P} = \bar{A}$ and $M_P^2 = S_E^2$.

and a presentation of some corresponding estimates.[9] This section will merely summarize some of the results of this analysis and rely mainly on the simpler measures given in the tables of the present report.

The mean errors of the annual forecasts in our collection are given in Tables 4, 5, and 6 above. They vary greatly in size relative to the average magnitude of the changes that the forecasters tried to predict (compare columns 1 and 7 in Table 4) and also relative to the corresponding mean absolute errors. Tests of the statistical significance of the mean errors are presented elsewhere (see the reference in note 9). They confirm that the relative importance of bias varies substantially among forecasts from different sources and for different variables. Thus the tests give considerable evidence of bias in some of the GNP forecasts, but very little indication of significant bias in the industrial production forecasts. The differences among forecasters are probably less meaningful; they cannot be ascribed entirely to the variation in ability or technique because the periods covered are not identical for all the sets.[10] In general, however, these tests lack conclusiveness, since the periods covered by our data are short and, hence, the samples of observations per forecast set are small.

A point of interest in the GNP forecasts is that they generally start from estimates of current levels that are too low. The mean errors in these estimates (ECP) are negative for all forecast sets (Table 4, column 8, lines 1–8). This is presumably due in part to the forecasters' reliance on early figures that are often revised upward during the year to which the forecasts refer.[11] The base values for industrial production, a variable for which such revisions are less frequent and less important, seem to be in most cases somewhat overestimated (Table 4, column 8, lines 16–22). In any event, the base estimates are often substantially biased and, consistent with this, the elements of bias tend to be larger in the level forecasts than in the corresponding change forecasts.

[9] Jacob Mincer and Victor Zarnowitz, "The Evaluation of Economic Forecasts" (forthcoming).

[10] For example, the forecast set A for GNP shows a strong bias, with the squared mean error $\bar{E}^2$ accounting for approximately 40 per cent of the total $M_p{}^2$ (see note 8 for the formula used). But this feature of set A is due mainly to large underestimation errors in the early postwar years (see first section in Chapter 3).

[11] Possibly some forecasters are aware of this bias in their estimates and try to compensate for it implicitly in their change predictions rather than explicitly by correcting their ECP figures. This assumption would be consistent with one of our forecast sets, in which the base levels are underestimated but the changes in GNP are overestimated (Table 4, line 7).

Other studies have suggested that forecasters generally underestimate both rises and declines in the predicted series.[12] In this case, the *absolute* average and the variance of the predicted changes would be smaller than those of the actual changes, but there need be no bias, in the specific sense of a significant difference between the arithmetic averages of predictions and realizations. Indeed, underestimation of changes would not constitute a systematic error that forecasters could or should guard against if it were merely the result of forecasters failing to predict random variations in the actual values. A forecaster who ignored only such variations and succeeded in predicting all other changes would have done as well as could be hoped for, yet his forecast would have a variance smaller than that of the actual values and, in this sense, would necessarily "underestimate" the observed changes.[13]

As this illustrates, it is important to recognize that forecasting errors which can be traced directly to short random movements must be regarded as unavoidable. Thus, a sudden outbreak of war or a strike started without warning are events that an economic forecaster can hardly be expected to predict (though his job certainly does include an evaluation of the effects of such events, once known, on the economy). To put it differently, in principle the requirement of a good forecast is that it predict well the systematic movements of the given variable, not that it predict the actual values, since random elements are virtually always present in economic time series.

Underestimation of changes would have a different meaning if the changes pertained to longer cyclical movements, not just to short irregular variations. This result could come about if forecast errors varied systematically with the values predicted so as to yield underestimates at high and overestimates at low levels. Predictions with this property would have a larger over-all error than predictions which are independent of levels, hence elimination of this type of systematic

[12] Franco Modigliani and Owen H. Sauerlander, "Economic Expectations and Plans of Firms in Relation to Short-Term Forecasting," in *Short-Term Economic Forecasting*, Studies in Income and Wealth 17, Princeton for NBER, 1955, Table 8 (based on the *Fortune* and Dun & Bradstreet Surveys), pp. 288–289; Henri Theil, *Economic Forecasts and Policy*, Amsterdam, 1958, Chapters III–V.

[13] Consider the equation $A_t = a + bP_t + u_t$. Unbiased, efficient forecasts require that $a = 0$, $b = 1$, and that $u_t$ be a random, nonautocorrelated variable with mean zero. In this case, the variance of $A$ will equal the sum of the variances of $P$ and of $u$.

underestimation error must be viewed as desirable.[14] But again, errors of this kind do not necessarily involve a bias, that is, a discrepancy between long-run averages computed with regard to sign.[15] This can be perceived intuitively by visualizing forecasts that result in a series with cyclical movements around a trend smaller than those actually recorded, but with a correct estimate of the trend itself. Here, then, is a type of systematic (and potentially serious) error which is not encompassed by the usual statistical definition of bias.[16]

Have the forecasters represented in our collection tended to underestimate changes of either the random or the systematic kind, or both? The hypothesis that forecasters manage to reproduce the time path of the predicted series in some smoothed form receives little support from the materials under review. Actual changes are in fact usually reduced in the forecasts, but not regularly in both the upward and downward direction as the hypothesis would imply.[17] The forecast errors are by no means limited to the random components of the series, though such irregular movements doubtless account for a large part of the fore-

[14] If $P_t$ and $E_t$ are correlated, $b \neq 1$ in the relation $A_t = a + bP_t + u_t$ (in the case of underestimation of systematic changes, $b > 1$). The adjusted forecast $P_t^* = a + bP_t$ would be an improvement on the original forecast $P_t$, whenever the expected values of $a$ and $b$ deviate from zero and unity, respectively. Thus, if $b \neq 1$ then the variance of $E_t$ is larger than that of $u_t$ (i.e., $S_E^2 > S_u^2$), since $S_E^2 = S_u^2 + (1 - b)^2 S_P^2$ (where $S_P^2$ is the variance of $P_t$).

[15] From the formulas for $M_P^2$ and $S_E^2$ in notes 8 and 14, it follows that the mean square error can be decomposed into three parts:

$$M_P^2 = \bar{E}^2 + S_E^2 = (\bar{P} - \bar{A})^2 + (1 - b) S_P^2 + S_u^2.$$

In unbiased forecasts, $\bar{P} = \bar{A}$ and the first component of $M_P^2$ is zero; but the second component will be positive, unless $b = 1$ (it is an increasing function of the deviations of $b$ from zero). It may be noted that this decomposition is equivalent to one of the two forms introduced in Henri Theil, op. cit., pp. 34–39.

[16] One must remember, however, that bias is a possible property of sample estimates referring to some population or aggregate of phenomena to be studied; hence, what bias is depends on the definition of that aggregate. If a good reason existed to treat different ranges of the series as belonging to different "populations," then bias in the strict sense could no longer be excluded in the above situation. For then the ranges would in effect be viewed as separate variables, and underestimation of one set of values (say, the high levels) would constitute one case of bias, while overestimation of the other set (low levels) would constitute another. In each range, predictions would differ on the average from realizations both for levels and changes.

[17] Presumably, smoothing out the irregular movements would work in both directions alike and not affect systematically the mean of the changes over time (this assumes that such movements themselves have a zero mean).

casters' difficulties.[18] As was shown in Chapter 3, forecast errors tend to differ depending on cyclical phase, with large underestimates being concentrated mainly in early expansion periods, which are typically periods of high growth rates.

Actually, it was primarily the increases in GNP that were underestimated in the forecasts reviewed, not the decreases (as will be demonstrated in the section that follows). Underestimation of increases alone would be sufficient to produce the observed result that the predicted *levels* of GNP, which is a series with an upward trend, were on the average too low (note the predominance of negative signs in column 6 of Table 4).[19] The same applies to the finding that, in terms of averages taken without regard to sign, actual changes exceeded predicted changes for twelve of the fifteen forecast sets recorded in Table 4 (columns 1–2). It is only when increases and decreases are treated separately that one can obtain meaningful indications of a downward bias in the forecasts—an underestimation of growth.

### UNDERESTIMATION OF GROWTH

Forecasters often regard themselves as "conservative" or "cautious." If this means cautious in appraising growth prospects, the results of our analysis bear out this view.

Chart 4 presents scatter diagrams for selected sets of annual forecasts, which relate the actual to the predicted changes. The chart is followed by a key, which is self-explanatory.

Because of the prevalence of upward trends in such series as GNP, personal consumption, and industrial production, the bulk of the observations in the corresponding scatters fall into the first quadrant

[18] The proportion $S_u{}^2/M_P{}^2$ in the GNP and industrial production forecasts (see note 15 for the underlying decomposition of $M_P{}^2$) is very seldom less than 0.5 and often as high as 0.9 or more (in which case, the other "systematic" components of $M_P{}^2$ are actually unlikely to be significant). However, it should be noted that the $u$'s are here simply the residuals from the regression of $A_t$ on $P_t$, i.e., that part of $A_t$ which the "predictor" $P_t$ was unable to account for; they need not be in fact purely random and nonautocorrelated.

[19] When increases are underestimated, the future levels of the series will also as a rule be underestimated. (This follows necessarily if the current position is known or itself understated.) On the other hand, underestimation of *decreases* would tend to result in *over*estimation of levels. Since rises are more frequent than declines in the series considered here, errors relating to rises, if sufficiently systematic and large, are likely to dominate the over-all result.

# CHART 4

## Scatter Diagrams of Relations Between Predicted and Actual Changes, Selected Annual Forecasts of Four Aggregative Variables, 1953–63

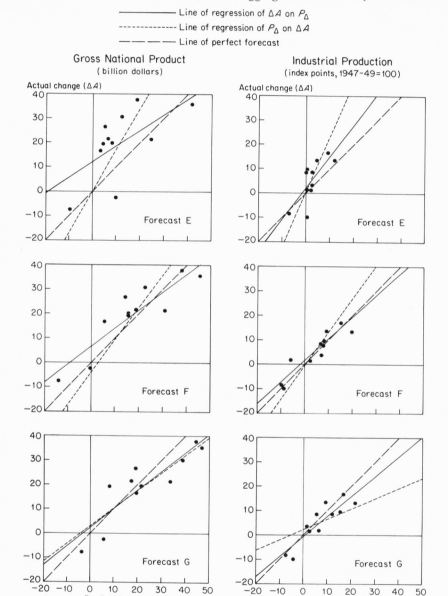

# CHART 4 (concluded)

## Personal Consumption
(billion dollars)

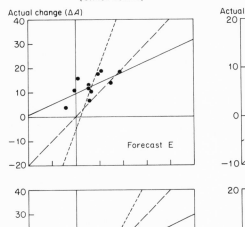

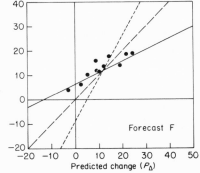

## Plant and Equipment Outlays
(billion dollars)

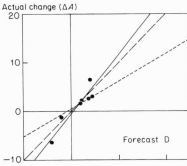

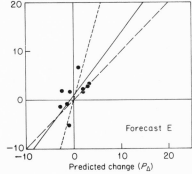

## KEY

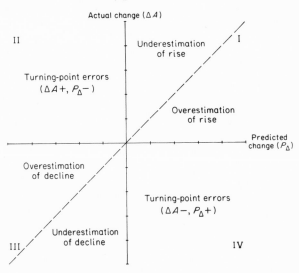

(where the actual and predicted changes, $\Delta A$ and $P_\Delta$, are both positive). That is, few declines occurred in the annual values of GNP and few were expected, hence there are relatively few points in the other quadrants. Also, there are often more points above than below the 45° line of perfect forecasts in quadrant I. This means that underestimates of increases are more frequent than overestimates.

Reflecting these characteristics of the scatters, the regression lines in Chart 4 run, in large part, through the areas of underestimation of changes.[20] This, however, is by no means always true, as illustrated in the diagrams for forecasts G where the overestimates carry more weight than the underestimates.

For series that are more volatile, such as the plant and equipment outlays, the scatters show no distinct concentrations of points in any single quadrant. Increases are less dominant here and less confidently predicted. Sometimes declines have been expected instead, giving rise to turning point errors in quadrant II; at other times, declines have been correctly predicted (quadrant III). The combination of predicted rises and actual declines is not recorded in our graph for the plant and equipment outlays (quadrant IV is empty there) but a few examples of such turning-point errors are found in other investment forecasts. As this illustration suggests, forecasts of such variables show little evidence of biases but also low correlations with the observed changes.

While the results for the different forecast sets vary in several respects, including the significance of the regression estimates, as would be expected, it is worth noting that in most cases the regressions of the actual on the predicted changes show positive intercepts and slopes less than one (see the solid regression lines in Chart 4).

Table 7 summarizes the distributions of errors in the forecasts of annual changes according to whether they represented overestimates, underestimates, or turning-point (directional) errors. It confirms that forecasters frequently underrated the increases in GNP, while displaying no such tendency in regard to decreases.

In interpreting this asymmetry, it is necessary to recall that the recent recessions in the United States have been sufficiently mild and short to cause only very small declines, or merely retardations of

[20] Note in particular the diagram for the industrial production forecast E, in which the scatter and both regression lines clearly indicate a tendency to underestimate increases and decreases.

### TABLE 7

*Forecasts of Annual Changes in Four Comprehensive Aggregates:*
*Distribution by Type of Change and Type of Error, 1952-63*

| Line | Type of Change[a] | Number of Forecasts of Annual Changes | | | | Probability of at Least as Many Under-estimates[e] |
|---|---|---|---|---|---|---|
| | | Total (1) | Under-estimates[b] (2) | Over-estimates[c] (3) | Turning-Point Errors[d] (4) | (5) |
| | | *Gross National Product (8)*[f] | | | | |
| 1. | All observations | 78 | 46 | 25 | 7 | .008 |
| 2. | Increases | 64 | 43 | 21 | 0 | .004 |
| 3. | Decreases | 14 | 3 | 4 | 7 | .756 |
| | | *Personal Consumption Expenditures (4)*[f] | | | | |
| 4. | All observations[g] | 39 | 26 | 10 | 3 | .006 |
| | | *Gross Private Domestic Investment (3)*[f] | | | | |
| 5. | All observations | 28 | 12 | 12 | 4 | .581 |
| 6. | Increases | 18 | 8 | 7 | 3 | .500 |
| 7. | Decreases | 10 | 4 | 5 | 1 | .746 |
| | | *Industrial Production (7)*[f] | | | | |
| 8. | All observations | 70 | 37 | 26 | 7 | .104 |
| 9. | Increases | 57 | 28 | 23 | 6 | .288 |
| 10. | Decreases | 13 | 9 | 3 | 1 | .073 |

[a]Increases and decreases refer to the direction of changes in the actual values (first estimates for the given series).

[b]Predicted change is less than actual change $(P_{\triangle (t+1)} < \triangle A_{t+1})$.

[c]Predicted change exceeds actual change $(P_{\triangle (t+1)} > \triangle A_{t+1})$.

[d]Sign $P_{\triangle (t+1)} \neq$ sign $\triangle A_{t+1}$.

[e]Based on the proportion of all observations, other than those with turning-point errors, accounted for by the underestimates (i.e., col. 2 divided by the difference between col. 1 and col. 4). Probabilities taken from Harvard Computation Laboratory's *Tests of the Cumulative Binomial Probability Distribution*, Cambridge, Mass., 1955.

[f]The figure in parentheses is the number of forecast sets covered.

[g]All observed changes are increases.

growth, in the *annual* values of GNP. According to early estimates, declines occurred in 1953–54 and 1957–58.[21] On the former occasion most forecasts showed larger declines than actually occurred, and on the latter most of them missed the downturn. In the years when GNP increased, on the other hand, underestimates were almost twice as frequent as overestimates (see Table 7, lines 2 and 3). In forecasts of personal consumption expenditures, a series which has risen steadily in recent years, errors of underestimation also prevail (Table 7, line 4).

In contrast, overestimates are about as frequent as underestimates in forecasts of gross private investment (lines 5–7). In this series the trend is much weaker than in the others, and the cyclical and irregular movements are relatively stronger. Also, for industrial production, a series with more pronounced fluctuations than those in GNP in current dollars and with a weaker trend, the forecasts show less tendency to underestimate increases. On the other hand, the production index declined much more in recessions than GNP did, and its contractions were in fact very often understated (Table 7, lines 8–10).

In short, these results suggest that the notion that forecasters tend to underestimate changes in general—that is, increases as well as decreases, short fluctuations as well as longer trends—is a gross oversimplification. Important asymmetries seem to exist here between errors in predicting upward and downward changes and also between forecasts for series with strong growth trends and others.[22]

Examination of forecasts of other GNP components yields additional evidence that is consistent with the hypothesis of underestimation of growth. For all the major expenditure components taken together, increases were underestimated nearly half the time and overestimated more than one-third of the time, while turning-point errors account for the remaining one-sixth of these observations. Decreases were underestimated about as often as overestimated; they were also, on the whole, just as frequently missed, but the proportion of these turning-

[21] Subsequent revisions converted the declines of GNP in 1953–54 and 1957–58 into small *increases* (see Table 2, lines 1–2, columns 2 and 6).

[22] The last column of Table 7 lists the probabilities of observing at least as many underestimates as shown by the forecasts in question. These are derived under certain highly simplified assumptions which permit application of the binomial distribution: that the forecasts are independent and the chances of under- and overestimation are equal in all cases with no turning-point errors. These assumptions can be questioned and the tests cannot be interpreted in any strict sense, but the results are suggestive in the context of the preceding observations.

point errors varies greatly (set B missed half the declines, set F just one-sixth).

As this indicates, all types of error are well represented in these forecasts, which reflects in part the diverse behavior patterns of the series concerned. The prevalence of negative signs among the mean errors (Table 5, col. 2, and Table 6, columns 2 and 4) is due not simply to underestimation of changes but to a combination of factors: over 70 per cent of the observations relate to *increases* in the series, where underestimation is common; and most of the turning-point errors are negative, being false signals of declines.[23]

To conclude, asymmetries in the distribution by type of errors associated with increases and decreases cast doubt upon the simple hypothesis of general underestimation of changes, but there is considerable support for the idea that forecasters tend to underrate increases or growth of comprehensive economic aggregates. As a closely related point, there is also some direct evidence that underestimation occurs primarily in certain phases of business cycles, particularly in the early upswing (see Table 3 and text above). Such patterns probably would not be observed if this type of error applied merely, or even largely, to short erratic changes.

### TURNING-POINT ERRORS

Many economic time series, and especially those of comprehensive coverage, show strong systematic movements of substantial duration—trends and specific cycles. They are positively autocorrelated, often to a high degree. These observations led to the now widely held idea that it should be rather easy to predict a continuation of the rise or fall in these series; to forecast correctly the end of the current movement or phase appears to mark a more meaningful predictive success.

To appraise the performance of forecasts with respect to turning-point errors, one must compare the signs of predicted and actual changes. A forecast for any future period is based on the estimate of the current value of the series, not on the past forecast that has already been superseded by the intervening information; hence forecasts

[23] Errors of change (defined as the forecast minus the actual figure) are negative when increases are underestimated or decreases are overestimated and when the predicted change is negative and the actual one is positive. In our samples, the totals of such cases are typically greater than those of the converse cases in which the errors of change are positive.

made at successive points of time do not form a continuous series. Inferences from level forecasts treated as a series can easily be wrong, particularly on turning-point errors.[24]

Suppose a series rises, declines, and rises again in three consecutive years, while forecasts indicate three increases. Looking at the levels, one may conclude that the forecaster missed two turning points, a peak and a trough. Looking at the patterns of change, which are $+ - +$ for $A_t$ and $+ + +$ for $P_t$, one finds a single directional error, relating to the change between years 1 and 2. Actually, only one turning-point error was made, since the forecaster knew at the end of year 2 that a decline had taken place and decided that it would be reversed the following year. In short, to determine whether a turning point has been forecast, one must compare the forecast change with the preceding actual change, not with the preceding forecast change.

In evaluating turning-point errors, two questions must be asked: (1) How often do turning points occur that have not been predicted? (2) How often do predicted turns actually occur? Accordingly, there are two basic types of error: missed turns and false signals. In the preceding paragraph, an example of a missed turn was provided. A false signal would be given in the case of reversed patterns: $+ + +$ for $A_t$ and $+ - +$ for $P_t$.[25]

In addition to the two types of error, there are two types of correct forecasts. One is when a turning point (TP) was predicted and it did

---

[24] Consider the following tabulation on the actual ($A$) and predicted ($P$) values of industrial production. It will be noted that the troughs (T) fall in the first half of 1958 for $A$ and in the second half of 1958 for $P$—an apparent lag of the latter behind the former. But the reversal of sign from minus to plus occurred at the same time in both the actual and the predicted change, which indicates the absence of a real lag (the directional change is denoted by *). The important point here is that such a situation can readily be produced by underestimation of changes on both sides of the turning point.

| Date ($t$) | $A_t$ | $(A_t - A_{t-1})$ | $P_t$ | $(P_t - A_{t-1})$ |
|---|---|---|---|---|
| 2nd half 1957 | 142 | | | |
| 1st half 1958 | 129 (T) | −13 | 138 | −4 |
| 2nd half 1958 | 138 | +9* | 130 (T) | +1* |
| 1st Q 1959 | 145 | +7 | 143 | +5 |

[25] Reversing the order of presentation used above, one can say that type I error arises when a turning point was predicted but did not occur; type II error, when a turning point was not predicted but did occur. This parallels the familiar statistical dichotomy of first-kind and second-kind errors, the former consisting of an incorrect rejection, the latter of an incorrect acceptance of the null hypothesis (which is here represented by a forecast of no directional change).

occur; the other, when no TP was predicted and none occurred. Thus there are four basic possibilities which can be arranged in a $2 \times 2$ table as follows. ($N$ refers to the absence, $T$ to the presence of a turning point. The first letter refers to actual values, the second to forecasts.)

| Forecast / Actual | No TP | TP |
|---|---|---|
| No TP | $NN$ | $NT$ |
| TP | $TN$ | $TT$ |

The number of correct forecasts is the sum of the diagonal frequencies: $NN + TT$. False signals are represented by $NT$ and missed turns by $TN$. To compute the proportion of the former, one should use as a base the number of all predicted turns. This yields the ratio $\bar{E}_{T1} = \dfrac{NT}{NT + TT}$. In the proportion of missed turns, on the other hand, the base is the number of all recorded turns $\bar{E}_{T2} = \dfrac{TN}{TN + TT}$. These proportions of turning-point errors are analogous to mean errors, hence the choice of symbols.[26]

If forecasters relied mainly on trend projections, their record would be relatively good on false warnings and poor on missed turns.

The tendency for a comprehensive aggregate such as GNP to grow most of the time is well known to economic observers; hence few reversals of direction from one year to another are recorded for this series, and also few are predicted (note the high proportions of $NN$ in Table 8, column 2). False signals are particularly infrequent. Only two are listed for the annual GNP predictions, and these refer to the first two years covered, 1947 and 1948, when an early postwar slump was still widely anticipated (see column 7, line 1).

For variables with stronger cyclical and irregular components, turning-point predictions should, and probably will, be more numerous. Although the chances that a predicted turn will actually occur are

[26] Assign to each case in the category $NT$ the value 1 and to each case in the category $TT$ the value 0; the mean of these values is $\bar{E}_{T1}$ and their variance is $S^2_{T1} = \bar{E}_{T1}(1 - \bar{E}_{T1})$. Similarly, assign to each instance of $TN$ the value 1 and to each instance of $TT$ the value 0; here the mean of the resulting scores is $\bar{E}_{T2}$ and their variance is $S^2_{T2} = \bar{E}_{T2}(1 - \bar{E}_{T2})$.

## TABLE 8

### Frequency of Turning Points and Errors in Annual Forecasts of GNP and Industrial Production, 1947-63

| Line | Fore-Cast Set[a] | Period Covered | Number of Years[b] Covered (NN+TT+TN+NT) (1) | Number of Years[b] With No TP Observed or Predicted (NN) (2) | Number of Turning Points[b] Observed (TT+TN) (3) | Number of Turning Points[b] Predicted (TT+NT) (4) | Number of Turning Points[b] Correctly Predicted (TT) (5) | Number of Turning Points[b] Missed (TN) (6) | Number of Turning Points[b] Falsely Predicted (NT) (7) | Percentage[b] of Observed Turns Missed[c] ($\bar{E}_{T2}$) (8) | Percentage[b] of Predicted Turns False[d] ($\bar{E}_{T1}$) (9) |
|---|---|---|---|---|---|---|---|---|---|---|---|
| | | | | | *Gross National Product* | | | | | | |
| 1. | A | 1947-49, 1954-63 | 13 | 8 | 3 | 4 | 2 | 1 | 2 | 33 | 50 |
| 2. | B | 1953-63 | 11 | 9 | 2 | 1 | 1 | 1 | 0 | 50 | 0 |
| 3. | C | 1958-63 | 6 | 5 | 1 | 0 | 0 | 1 | 0 | 100 | 0 |
| 4. | D | 1956-63 | 8 | 7 | 1 | 0 | 0 | 1 | 0 | 100 | 0 |
| 5. | E | 1953-63 | 11 | 9 | 2 | 1 | 1 | 1 | 0 | 50 | 0 |
| 6. | F | 1953-63 | 11 | 9 | 2 | 2 | 2 | 0 | 0 | 0 | 0 |
| 7. | G | 1953-63[e] | 11 | 9 | 2 | 1 | 1 | 1 | 0 | 50 | 0 |
| 8. | H | 1954-63 | 10 | 8 | 2 | 1 | 1 | 1 | 0 | 50 | 0 |
| | | | | | *Index of Industrial Production* | | | | | | |
| 9. | A | 1947-49, 1954-63 | 13 | 9 | 3 | 4 | 3 | 0 | 1 | 0 | 25 |
| 10. | C | 1958-63 | 6 | 4 | 1 | 2 | 1 | 0 | 1 | 0 | 50 |
| 11. | D | 1947-63 | 17 | 10 | 4 | 6 | 3 | 1 | 3 | 25 | 50 |
| 12. | E | 1951-63 | 13 | 10 | 3 | 1 | 1 | 2 | 0 | 67 | 0 |
| 13. | F | 1953-63 | 11 | 8 | 2 | 3 | 2 | 0 | 1 | 0 | 33 |
| 14. | G | 1953-63 | 11 | 9 | 2 | 2 | 2 | 0 | 0 | 0 | 0 |
| 15. | H | 1954-63 | 10 | 7 | 2 | 3 | 2 | 0 | 1 | 0 | 33 |

(continued)

## TABLE 8 (concluded)

| Line | Fore-Cast Set[a] | Period Covered | Number of Years[b] | | Number of Turning Points[b] | | | | | Percentage[b] of | |
|---|---|---|---|---|---|---|---|---|---|---|---|
| | | | Covered (NN+TT+TN+NT) (1) | With No TP Observed or Predicted (NN) (2) | Observed (TT+TN) (3) | Predicted (TT+NT) (4) | Correctly Predicted (TT) (5) | Missed (TN) (6) | Falsely Predicted (NT) (7) | Observed Turns Missed[c] ($\bar{E}_{T_2}$) (8) | Predicted Turns False[d] ($\bar{E}_{T_1}$) (9) |
| | | | | | | | *Summary* | | | | |
| 16. | 8 forecasts of GNP[f] | | 81 | 64 | 15 | 10 | 8 | 7 | 2 | 46.7 | 20.0 |
| 17. | 7 forecasts of indus. prod.[g] | | 81 | 57 | 17 | 21 | 14 | 3 | 7 | 17.6 | 33.3 |

[a]The forecasts are described in the text above and Tables 1 and 2. The total period covered by the forecast is used in each case.

[b]For symbols used, see text.

[c]Column 6 as per cent of column 3.

[d]Column 7 as per cent of column 4.

[e]Based on forecasts in constant dollars, as reported, compared with the corresponding actual values.

[f]Figures in columns 1-7 are totals of the corresponding entries on lines 1-8.

[g]Figures in columns 1-7 are totals of the corresponding entries on lines 9-15.

greater here, there are likely to be more false warnings as well. This may help explain the fact that among the annual forecasts of industrial production from the same sources the frequency of false signals is higher than among the GNP forecasts (column 9, lines 16–17).[27]

According to Table 8, forecasters of GNP seem to have failed to predict almost one-half of the turning points that did occur (column 8, line 16). But this hit-and-miss record appears much worse than it is. All these errors refer to the 1957–58 decline, which was very small to begin with in the early annual GNP estimates and was ultimately replaced by a small increase in the current, revised figures (see Table 8, lines 1–2, column 6). Thus, had we used the current instead of the former estimates in our error computations, the record of these forecasts would have been much better on this occasion.

On the other hand, forecasters generally did predict a decline in GNP in 1954 and, until very recently, data bore them out on this score.[28] However, according to the latest revised figures released in July 1965, there was apparently no decrease in the annual GNP series between 1953 and 1954 after all, but rather a minuscule increase (see Table 2, column 2). In this case, then, forecasters were "right" about the sign of change in this series according to all but the most recent data. All this illustrates mainly the highly uncertain nature of directional comparisons when these are applied to a series subject to relatively small short-period changes and revisions large enough to alter the sign of such changes.

Forecasts of industrial production show only three "misses" on seventeen occasions (column 5, line 17). This gives a smaller proportion of errors than that shown for GNP; the results here are more

[27] Of the seven errors of this kind for the industrial production forecasts, five refer to 1961 and one each to 1948 and 1963. In all these cases, declines were predicted but increases actually occurred.

[28] This is shown in Table 2, column 2, where the predicted changes are all negative and so is the actual change according to the first GNP estimates. Later estimates whittled down this decline; those available in May 1965, for example, show a change of −$2.3 billion instead of −$7.7 billion, which is the early figure listed in Table 2, line 1.

valid in the sense that they do not depend on the vintage or revisions of the data.[29]

For both GNP and industrial production, all false signals are predictions of peaks (declines) that never materialized; and all missed turns are peaks, i.e., increases were predicted but declines were posted (at least according to the early measurements used here). This situation is also reflected in the distributions of turning-point errors by type of change in the observed figures, as shown in Table 7 above.[30]

These results indicate that the main difficulty in predicting reversals of the economy in the postwar period was with downturns rather than upturns. This is certainly not surprising. In recent times, business contractions have been relatively mild and brief and have been widely expected to be so. They varied much less in duration than expansions did. It was generally assumed that antirecessionary policies would be used to attenuate and cut short any declines in aggregate economic activity. On the other hand, the success of policies designed to steady and lengthen expansions was probably more difficult to gauge.

Furthermore, recent business cycle peaks have occurred early enough in the year to be recognized as such by the end of the year, which is the time when the annual forecasts are made.[31] Thus forecasts for 1954, 1958, and 1961 reflected the widespread assumption that the contractions then in process had already run most of their course.[32]

In short, it is demonstrably quite difficult to appraise annual forecasts

[29] Of these three errors, two refer to the late Korean period (1952) when increases were predicted but declines occurred. One "miss" in the opposite direction is recorded for 1958.

[30] According to Table 7, column 4, all turning-point errors in GNP forecasts since 1952 were associated with declines in GNP. These represent missed peaks. In the industrial production forecasts, six errors were associated with increases and one with a decrease; the former are false signals of peaks, the latter is a missed peak. (Note that Table 7 excludes forecasts made before 1952, which are covered in Table 8.)

[31] According to the National Bureau chronology of business cycle turns, the last three peaks are dated July 1953, July 1957, and May 1960. The corresponding dates of specific peaks in GNP (whether measured in current or constant dollars) are II Q 1953, III Q 1957, and II Q 1960. The downturns in industrial production were considerably earlier on two occasions (February 1957 and January 1960).

[32] This does not imply, however, that the dates of the coming troughs were well specified in these forecasts; it does not even necessarily mean that the dates of the troughs were predicted better than those of the peaks. No such inferences can be made with any assurance from an analysis of annual forecasts; a year is simply too long a unit period for that.

with respect to their turning-point performance, especially for GNP. A year is too long a unit period for such an evaluation, since recessions have been short and mild enough to leave only an uncertain imprint upon the annual data. Nevertheless, an over-all survey suggests a positive answer to the question: Were turns predicted more frequently when observed turns occurred? The evidence lies in the concentration of the recent forecasts of directional change in the two periods during which recessions did actually occur (causing at least the early annual GNP estimates to decline), namely, in 1953–54 and 1957–58.

While this is believed to be a meaningful result in a practical sense, its statistical significance cannot be readily established. The double dichotomy of turning-point forecasts introduced earlier in this discussion invites the application of the familiar chi-square ($\chi^2$) test of independence.[33] When the data in Table 8 are pooled for either GNP or industrial production, high values of $\chi^2$ are obtained, whose acceptance would imply a refutation of the (null) hypothesis that the predicted turning points are randomly distributed.[34] However, such pooling of the data requires independence among the forecast sets, which cannot, in general, be assumed. Forecasters presumably influence each other in various ways and most agree that they do; indeed, the nature of their environment and efforts is such as to make this just about inevitable.

No estimate of the magnitude of these complex effects can be provided with reasonable assurance. Forecasts of the same series, if they are any good, must, of course, be positively correlated. In fact, the correlations among them are typically substantial, as would be expected: after all, these forecasts all draw in part on the same informa-

---

[33] In our notation, the difference of the cross products in the $2 \times 2$ table concerned is $d = NN \times TT - NT \times TN$. Let the marginal totals be $e = NN + NT$, $f = TN + TT$, $g = NN + TN$, and $h = NT + TT$; then $\chi^2 = \dfrac{d^2 n}{efgh}$ (where $n = e + f = g + h$). For small frequencies, the use of a continuous instead of a discontinuous distribution may considerably understate the probability of obtaining the given result by chance. An approximate allowance for this can be made by means of the "Yates' correction," which yields $\chi_{y}^2 = \dfrac{(d - n/2)^2 n}{efgh}$. See R. A. Fisher, *Statistical Methods for Research Workers*, 12th ed., New York, 1954, Chapter IV.

[34] The values of $\chi^2$ computed from the appropriate entries in lines 16 and 17 of Table 8 are: for GNP, 28.6; for industrial production, 35.7. The corresponding values of $\chi_{y}^2$ are 24.1 and 32.1. The probabilities of obtaining such results by chance are very small indeed (less than .001).

tion and knowledge about the past behavior of the given series and related variables. This holds even if the forecasters did not influence each other directly at all. Therefore, the effects of any such influences, whatever their cause (reputation of some leading experts, pressures to conform, contagious expectations, etc.), would probably be to strengthen the correlations that already exist. Lacking detailed insight into each forecaster's procedures, it seems impossible to separate the effects of the common data from those direct influences that are opposed to the hypothesis of forecasters' mutual independence.[35]

Comparison of forecasts does reveal considerable diversity, however, suggesting a large role for independent analysis and individual judgment, despite the undoubtedly important common elements (see, e.g., Chart 1). Pure imitation must be rare among self-respecting forecasters, and the observed similarities are usually partial and temporary. Pooling the forecasts from different sources, therefore, will presumably result in a certain effective increase in the number of independent observations. But this increase is certainly less than that implied in the simple sums used in the over-all $\chi^2$ test; hence the latter understates, by an unknown quantity, the probability of obtaining the observed results by chance. Consequently, the results of such tests (see footnote 34) may at best be suggestive, but cannot be interpreted in any strict sense.

If the periods covered were longer, so that the numbers of observations were sufficiently large, the tests of whether predicted turns are randomly distributed or associated with actual turns could be usefully applied to data for each separate forecast set. As it is, however, the turning-point frequencies for the individual sets included in Table 8 are too small to permit reliable tests of this sort.

[35] One might speculate that common successes are attributable to the use of similar, valid methods in handling the same data, while common errors are due to direct influences such as the spread of plausible expectations that proved wrong. But this need not be so. It is true, of course, that forecasts may share errors as well as successes; their concordance does not always signify a higher correlation with the actual outcomes. But it is possible for an analysis recognized as valid and used independently by many forecasters to lead occasionally to widespread errors; and, conversely, for an influential individual's view of the future, which was adopted by many, to prove right.

# 5

# TIME SPAN OF FORECASTS
# AND PREDICTIVE ACCURACY

AVERAGE ERRORS OF FORECASTS WITH DIFFERENT SPANS:
GNP AND INDUSTRIAL PRODUCTION

Five of our forecast sets provide chains of predictions made at a given date for two or more successive periods, e.g., for the first and second halves, or the four quarters, of the coming year. These data have been used to analyze the performance of forecasts over different intervals between the current base and the future target (which is called the *span* of the forecast).

The evidence shows clearly that the average errors of short-term forecasts increase as the span increases. Table 9 demonstrates this for predictions of changes in GNP and industrial production, expressed in units of the predicted series.[1] But the decreasing accuracy of longer-span forecasts could also be shown in terms of the level errors or the relative change errors (predicted relative change minus actual relative change). The progression to larger errors appears in all summary measures (means, standard deviations, and root mean square errors) and in forecasts of variables with quite different characteristics.

The increase in the mean absolute errors with the extension of the predictive span is in general steady and substantial, though in some cases it weakens considerably at the longer end of the range, between a year and eighteen months (Table 9, lines 1–5 and 11–15). There can be no doubt that the predictions are considerably more accurate, in absolute terms, over the next three months than over the next six, and more accurate again over six months than over nine or twelve.

---

[1] The error of predicted change is $E_{\Delta(t+m)} = P_{\Delta(t+m)} - \Delta A_{t+m}$, where $m$ is the span of the forecast. See footnote 1, Chapter 4, which refers to the case where $m = 1$ year.

Averages taken with regard to sign (lines 6–10 and 16–20) are negative for all GNP and industrial production forecasts with spans of six months or more, except for set G. The absolute values of these arithmetic means tend to increase with the span of forecast in all cases.

TABLE 9

*Average Errors in Forecasts of Changes in GNP*
*and Industrial Production for Spans from Three to Eighteen Months,*
*1947-63*

| Line | Forecast Set[a] | Span of Forecast (Months) | | | | | |
|---|---|---|---|---|---|---|---|
| | | Three (1) | Six (2) | Nine (3) | Twelve (4) | Fifteen (5) | Eighteen (6) |
| | | *Gross National Product: Mean Absolute Errors (billion dollars)* | | | | | |
| 1. | A | | 10.4 | | 17.6 | | |
| 2. | E | | 11.9 | | 20.1 | | |
| 3. | C[b] | 5.0 | 8.3 | 9.6 | 12.2 | 15.1 | |
| 4. | D | 5.0 | 9.8 | 10.0 | 11.0 | | |
| 5. | G[c] | 5.7 | 8.8 | 13.0 | 14.8 | 16.2 | 16.6 |
| | | *Gross National Product: Mean Errors (billion dollars)* | | | | | |
| 6. | A | | −5.8 | | −11.9 | | |
| 7. | E | | −6.6 | | −13.4 | | |
| 8. | C[b] | −1.7 | −3.0 | −3.4 | −3.9 | −10.1 | |
| 9. | D | 2.0 | −1.2 | −0.1 | −4.0 | | |
| 10. | G[c] | 4.9 | 6.8 | 9.7 | 10.0 | 13.8 | 13.6 |
| | | *Industrial Production: Mean Absolute Errors (1947-49 = 100)* | | | | | |
| 11. | A | | 5.9 | | 6.6 | | |
| 12. | E | | 5.2 | | 7.6 | | |
| 13. | C[b] | 2.1 | 4.3 | 5.0 | 5.7 | 7.1 | |
| 14. | D | 2.8 | 5.6 | 6.5 | 5.7 | | |
| 15. | G | 2.7 | 4.9 | 6.7 | 8.1 | 8.0 | 7.8 |
| | | *Industrial Production: Mean Errors (1947-49-100)* | | | | | |
| 16. | A | | −1.4 | | −1.8 | | |
| 17. | E | | −0.7 | | −2.0 | | |
| 18. | C[b] | 0.1 | −1.5 | −2.6 | −2.5 | −4.4 | |
| 19. | D | 0.4 | −1.0 | −1.3 | −1.9 | | |
| 20. | G | 2.0 | 2.9 | 3.9 | 4.3 | 5.0 | 5.1 |

*Notes to Table 9*

[a]The years covered and numbers of observations per span (in parentheses) are as follows: A: 1947-49, 1955-56, 1958-63 (11); C: 1958-63 (22, 20, 19, 13, and 7 for spans of three to fifteen months, respectively); D: 1959-63 (9); E: 1956, 1960-63 (5) for GNP; E: 1951-63 (13) for industrial production; G: 1955-63 (16) for GNP; G: 1956-63 (13) for industrial production.

[b]The entries on this line are not strictly comparable because some of the forecast chains are "incomplete," so that the number of observations for different spans varies (see note a). However, adjustments were made to allow for this by deleting selected observations, and the resulting differences were not large. The progression to larger errors associated with the increase in span was found to be characteristic of these forecasts regardless of the adjustments.

[c]Based on forecasts in constant prices, as reported.

## TYPES OF ERROR IN MULTIPERIOD FORECASTS

The minus signs of the arithmetic means in Table 9 reflect in large measure facts that are already familiar: most of the time the economy moved upward and forecasters expected it to do just that, but the predicted increases were often smaller than those that materialized on the record. However, a closer analysis of these forecasts discloses great variation in the type of error. The relative frequency of overestimates here is high, higher than in the annual forecasts, as shown by Table 10 which can be compared with Table 7. The frequency of directional errors is, as would be expected, much larger than in the annual forecasts (fewer directional changes occur in the annual than in the semiannual and quarterly figures, and fewer are also predicted).

In one set of forecasts, G, overestimates are actually more numerous than underestimates. These are highly optimistic predictions which show a tendency to overstate increases and to continue upward missing the decline. In view of the different characteristics of the forecasts in set G, the results for this set are shown separately in Table 10; the other sets, which have more in common, however, are handled as a group on this occasion.

As longer spans are taken, increases usually become more, and decreases less, numerous. The number of turning-point errors tends to decline, since fewer directional changes occur and fewer are expected over longer spans. In particular, the frequency of such errors is reduced

## TABLE 10

### Forecasts of GNP and Industrial Production with Different Spans: Distribution by Type of Change and Type of Error, 1947-63

| Line | Forecast Set[b] | Type of Change[c] | Number of Forecasts of Changes (all spans)[a] | | | | |
|------|------|------|------|------|------|------|------|
| | | | Total (1) | Under-esti-mates (2) | Over-esti-mates (3) | Turning-Point Errors (4) | Not Classified[d] (5) |
| | | *Gross National Product* | | | | | |
| 1. | A,C,D,E | Increases | 135 | 67 | 47 | 17 | 4 |
| 2. | A,C,D,E | Decreases | 14 | 4 | 2 | 7 | 1 |
| 3. | G | Increases | 76 | 16 | 55 | 4 | 1 |
| 4. | G | Decreases | 20 | 0 | 0 | 20 | 0 |
| | | *Industrial Production* | | | | | |
| 5. | A,C,D,E | Increases | 127 | 57 | 44 | 19 | 7 |
| 6. | A.C.D.E | Decreases | 37 | 11 | 3 | 9 | 14 |
| 7. | G | Increases | 50 | 18 | 29 | 3 | 0 |
| 8. | G | Decreases | 28 | 2 | 3 | 19 | 4 |

[a]Underestimates: predicted change is less than actual change. Overestimates: predicted change exceeds actual change. Turning-point errors: sign of predicted change differs from sign of actual change.

[b]This table covers the same sets of forecasts as Table 9. For detail on periods and numbers of observations, see Table 9, note a.

[c]Increases and decreases refer to the direction of changes in the actual values (first estimates for the given series).

[d]Line 1: Includes three forecasts of no change and one case of numerical agreement between predicted and reported change.

Line 2: Perfect numerical agreement between predicted and reported change.

Line 3: Prediction of no change.

Line 5: Includes three forecasts of no change, three instances of zero reported change (associated with forecasts of increases), and one case of numerical agreement between predicted and actual change.

Line 6: Includes seven forecasts of no change, six instances of zero reported change (associated with forecasts of decreases), and one case of numerical agreement between predicted and actual change.

Line 8: Includes three forecasts of no change and one instance of zero reported change (associated with a forecast of decrease).

because there are fewer *declines* to be overlooked. Underestimates can be expected to gain with the increase in span, since we have already observed that the larger rises are particularly apt to be understated and since, the further away his target, the more cautious the forecaster is likely to be. Just as uncertainty grows with the span, so does the forecaster's "caution," which leads him to avoid predicting large changes in general and to discount the more distant changes.[2]

Comparisons for all forecast sets and spans confirm that the longer the forecast, the smaller the share of turning-point errors and the larger the share of underestimates. Table 11 summarizes the evidence for all sets except G by contrasting the shortest (three- and six-month) with the longer (nine-, twelve-, and fifteen-month) forecasts. The percentages of underestimates are about 44 for the short and 55 for the longer forecasts of GNP. For industrial production, the corresponding figures are 41 and 53 per cent. The proportions of overestimates are essentially stable and those of turning-point errors drop sharply for the longer forecasts.[3]

Overestimates rather than underestimates prevail among those forecasts in set G which are associated with increases in GNP and industrial production. The forecasts for periods of decreases show here a very high concentration of turning-point errors; most of the errors of this type are due to failure to foresee downturns. As the spans increase, both over- and underestimates gain at the expense of turning-point errors, but the shifts in the distribution of errors by type are not large. In short, predictions from this source had a tendency to be overoptimistic regardless of span.[4]

### INTRAFORECAST CHANGES

Consider a chain of forecasts made at the time $t = 0$ for several future periods, say, the next four quarters. The predictions refer to levels at

---

[2] Although this argument seems plausible and in line with the notions of many forecasters, it is by no means conclusive. Greater uncertainty should show itself in lower probabilities being attached to forecasts rather than in biased forecasts. Regrettably, such probabilities are typically not stated by forecasters, who content themselves simply with point predictions.

[3] The latter fall from about 24 to 10 per cent for GNP and from 26 to 13 per cent for industrial production. These figures refer to all forecasts covered in Table 11, but the results for the dominant category of increases are similar.

[4] The proportions of under- and overestimates in the GNP forecasts of set G are: 13 and 52 per cent for the short, and 19 and 61 per cent for the longer predictions, respectively. For industrial production, the percentages are 25 and 42 for the short forecasts, 28 and 44 for the longer ones.

## TABLE 11

*Forecasts of GNP and Industrial Production with Spans of*
*Under and Over Six Months: Distribution by Type of*
*Change and Type of Error, 1947-63*

| Line | Span of Forecast[a] (months) | Type of Change[b] | Number of Forecasts of Changes | | | |
|---|---|---|---|---|---|---|
| | | | Total (1) | Under-estimates[c] (2) | Over-estimates[d] (3) | Turning-Point Errors[e] (4) |
| | | | *Gross National Product* | | | |
| 1. | 3 & 6 | Increases | 60 | 28 | 21 | 11 |
| 2. | 3 & 6 | Decreases | 11 | 3 | 2 | 6 |
| 3. | 9, 12, & 15 | Increases | 71 | 39 | 26 | 6 |
| 4. | 9, 12, & 15 | Decreases | 2 | 1 | 0 | 1 |
| | | | *Industrial Production* | | | |
| 5. | 3 & 6 | Increases | 52 | 22 | 20 | 10 |
| 6. | 3 & 6 | Decreases | 16 | 6 | 2 | 8 |
| 7. | 9, 12, & 15 | Increases | 68 | 35 | 24 | 9 |
| 8. | 9, 12, & 15 | Decreases | 7 | 5 | 1 | 1 |

[a]This table covers forecasts A, C, D, and E; these are the same as in Table 10, except that the "not classified" observations are excluded here. Set G is not covered (see text).

[b]Increases and decreases refer to the direction of changes in actual values.

[c]Predicted change is less than actual change.

[d]Predicted change exceeds actual change.

[e]Sign of predicted change differs from sign of actual change.

$t + m$ where $m$ = 3, 6, 9, 12 (months) and to changes over the intervals with increasing length, 0–3, 0–6, 0–9, and 0–12. Taking the differences between either the successive level or the successive change predictions (the results are the same), one gets the "intraforecast changes." These differences within a given chained forecast represent implicit predictions of changes over the successive *subperiods* covered. For example, in the four-quarter case, there are, in addition to the first change from the base (0–3), three intraforecast changes, 3–6, 6–9, and 9–12. They relate to slices of the future that are of equal length but are increasingly distant from the present. The sum of the errors of such marginal changes equals the error of the total change predicted over the entire span of the chain (here 0–12).[5]

Since this is so for each forecast chain, the well-known basic propositions about the (arithmetic) means and variances of sums apply here. Obviously, the sum of the mean errors of all subperiod changes must equal the mean error of the total change predicted per chain. Furthermore, the variance of the total change errors equals the sum of variances of the component change errors, plus the covariances. If the component errors were independent, the covariance terms would vanish. If these errors are correlated instead, which seems more likely, then the covariances will be nonzero, having the signs of the correlations among the errors.[6]

Unless the errors for the subperiods (the intraforecast changes) are *negatively* correlated to a sufficiently high degree,[7] they must clearly be cumulative. Since high negative correlations are unlikely, summary measures will probably show the errors of predicted changes to be larger, the greater the span: a longer forecast covers more of the subperiods over which the errors cumulate. Here, then, is another technical

---

[5] Every intraforecast change has the form $\Delta P_{ij} = P_{t+j} - P_{t+i}$, where $i$ and $j$ are two successive values assumed by the span $m$; e.g., the expression $(P_{t+6} - P_{t+3})$ would denote the difference between the simultaneously made predictions for two quarters and one quarter ahead. The error of $\Delta P_{ij}$ equals $E_{\Delta ij} = E_{t+j} - E_{t+i}$. The total change error $E_{\Delta(t+m)} = \Sigma E_{\Delta ij}$.

For brevity, let us illustrate these relations for a chain of only two forecasts for six and twelve months, and use simple self-explanatory symbols and subscripts, without the delta signs for changes. Then,

$$P_{0-12} = P_{0-6} + P_{6-12} \text{ and } E_{0-12} = E_{0-6} + E_{6-12} = (P_{0-6} - A_{0-6}) + (P_{6-12} - A_{6-12}).$$

[6] Returning to the simple example in footnote 5, let us adopt the shorthand subscripts 1 and 2 for the subperiods (0–6) and (6–12), respectively; the total period (0–12) can then be denoted by the subscript (1 + 2). In the usual symbols, the relation between the mean errors is

$$\bar{E}_{1+2} = \bar{E}_1 + \bar{E}_2,$$

and the relation between the variances is

$$\text{Var } (E_{1+2}) = \text{var } (E_1) + \text{var } (E_2) + 2 \text{ cov } (E_1, E_2) = S_{E_1}^2 + S_{E_2}^2 + 2rS_{E_1}S_{E_2},$$

where cov is covariance, var = $S^2$ is variance, and $r$ is the coefficient of correlation between the errors $E_1$ and $E_2$.

[7] For var $(E_{1+2})$ to be less than var $(E_1)$, the correlation between $E_1$ and $E_2$ must be such that (1) $r < 0$ and (2) $|r| > S_{E_2}/2S_{E_1}$. An analogous condition for var $(E_{1+2}) < \text{var } (E_2)$ is also readily derived from the relation given in footnote 6.

## TABLE 12

### Average Errors of Intraforecast Changes for GNP and Industrial Production, 1947-63

| Line | Forecast Set[a] | Interval of Predicted Change (months)[b] | | | | | | | |
|------|------|------|------|------|------|------|------|------|------|
| | | 0-3 (1) | 0-6 (2) | 3-6 (3) | 6-9 (4) | 6-12 (5) | 9-12 (6) | 12-15 (7) | 15-18 (8) |
| | | *Gross National Product: Mean Absolute Errors (billion dollars)* | | | | | | | |
| 1. | A | | 10.4 | | | 11.9 | | | |
| 2. | E | | 11.9 | | | 10.4 | | | |
| 3. | C[c] | 5.0 | | 5.4 | 4.7 | | 4.8 | 4.6 | |
| 4. | D | 5.0 | | 5.1 | 6.0 | | 5.6 | | |
| 5. | G[d] | 5.7 | | 4.3 | 6.5 | | 4.5 | 6.6 | 5.0 |
| | | *Gross National Product: Mean Errors (billion dollars)* | | | | | | | |
| 6. | A | | -5.8 | | | -6.1 | | | |
| 7. | E | | -6.6 | | | -6.8 | | | |
| 8. | C[c] | -1.7 | | -1.6 | -0.6 | | 0.8 | -2.3 | |
| 9. | D | 2.0 | | -3.3 | 1.1 | | -3.9 | | |
| 10. | G[d] | 4.9 | | 1.9 | 2.9 | | 0.3 | 3.8 | -0.2 |
| | | *GNP: Correlations of Predicted with Actual Changes* | | | | | | | |
| 11. | A | | .518 | | | .094 | | | |
| 12. | E | | .421 | | | .136 | | | |
| 13. | C[c] | .658 | | .217 | .164 | | .397 | .215 | |
| 14. | D | .234 | | .264 | .143 | | -.072 | | |
| 15. | G[d] | .649 | | .471 | .243 | | .282 | .197 | -.016 |
| | | *Industrial Production: Mean Absolute Errors (1947-49=100)* | | | | | | | |
| 16. | A | | 5.9 | | | 3.2 | | | |
| 17. | E | | 5.2 | | | 6.0 | | | |
| 18. | C[c] | 2.1 | | 3.5 | 3.4 | | 3.3 | 2.4 | |
| 19. | D | 2.8 | | 4.5 | 3.1 | | 3.6 | | |
| 20. | G | 2.7 | | 3.5 | 4.1 | | 3.9 | 4.0 | 3.6 |
| | | *Industrial Production: Mean Errors (1947-49=100)* | | | | | | | |
| 21. | A | | -1.4 | | | -0.4 | | | |
| 22. | E | | -0.7 | | | -1.3 | | | |
| 23. | C[c] | 0.1 | | -1.5 | -0.9 | | 1.6 | 0.7 | |
| 24. | D | 0.4 | | -1.4 | -0.3 | | -0.7 | | |
| 25. | G | 2.0 | | 0.9 | 1.0 | | 0.4 | 0.7 | 0.1 |

*(continued)*

TABLE 12 *(concluded)*

| Line | Forecast Set[a] | Interval of Predicted Change (months)[b] | | | | | | | |
|------|------|------|------|------|------|------|------|------|------|
| | | 0-3 (1) | 0-6 (2) | 3-6 (3) | 6-9 (4) | 6-12 (5) | 9-12 (6) | 12-15 (7) | 15-18 (8) |
| | *Industrial Production: Correlations of Predicted with Actual Changes* | | | | | | | | |
| 26. | A | | .486 | | | .576 | | | |
| 27. | E | | .192 | | | .434 | | | |
| 28. | C[c] | .800 | | .309 | .020 | | .335 | .500 | |
| 29. | D | .559 | | -.314 | .553 | | -.179 | | |
| 30. | G[d] | .831 | | .402 | .183 | | .211 | .329 | .325 |

[a]This table covers the same forecast sets as Table 9. For detail on periods and numbers of observations, see Table 9, note a.

[b]The current (base) period $t$ is marked 0, so that 0-3 denotes the three-month interval between $t$ and $(t + 3)$; 3-6, the three-month interval between $(t + 3)$ and $(t + 6)$; etc.

[c]The entries on this line are not strictly comparable because some of the forecast chains are "incomplete," so that the number of observations for different spans varies. See Table 9, note b.

[d]Based on forecasts in constant prices, as reported.

"explanation" of the already familiar inverse relationship between the span and the accuracy of forecasts.

Do the errors of the intraforecast changes tend to increase with the distance from the present? One might think that the change during, say, the first quarter in the chain (0–3) should be easier to predict than the change during the second quarter (3–6), and so on. However, in our data, errors of the implicit forecasts of such successive changes show no systematic increases. The absolute averages in Table 12 (lines 1–5 and 16–20) sometimes rise and sometimes decline; the differences among these figures are neither regular nor large.[8]

A recurrent bias in the chained forecasts could contribute to such results. In a simple hypothetical case, let the present level (assumed

[8] Other summary measures such as root mean square errors lead to similar conclusions. All these measures reflect both the central tendency and the dispersion of errors. The relations involving means and variances, which were set out earlier in this section, have clear implications for the mean square errors (it will be recalled that $M^2 = \bar{E}^2 + S_E^2$).

to be correctly estimated) be 100 and the predictions for two successive future periods be 103 and 106. If the actual levels turn out to be 104 and 108, then the errors of the two predictions are −1 and −2, increasing absolutely with the span. But the errors of the two intraforecast changes are the same (each being −1).[9]

As already noted, elements of persistent biases exist in the forecasts used here. Underestimation is common in all sets, except G in which overestimation prevails; these facts underlie the mean errors in Table 12 (lines 6–10 and 21–25). But this is by no means the whole story. The signs of the intraforecast change errors do vary in some chains. In most of these cases, the errors still cumulate because the negative correlation among them is not sufficiently high and they do not quite cancel each other out; and sometimes they do increase absolutely with the distance from the present.

It may be significant that intraforecast change errors showed more frequent and more sustained increases in the periods in which cyclical turning points occurred than at other times when movement continued in the same direction. In the latter sequences, errors were virtually always smaller and their variation was usually more irregular than in the former, as illustrated by the following tabulation of mean absolute errors (in billion dollars) for two sets of GNP forecasts (corresponding to lines 4 and 5 of Table 12):

| | Interval of Intraforecast Change (months) | | | | | |
|---|---|---|---|---|---|---|
| | 0–3 | 3–6 | 6–9 | 9–12 | 12–15 | 15–18 |
| *Forecasts D* | | | | | | |
| Periods with turning point (TP) | 4.6 | 5.5 | 7.3 | 9.5 | | |
| Periods without TP | 5.2 | 4.9 | 5.3 | 3.6 | | |
| *Forecasts G* | | | | | | |
| Periods with TP | 6.1 | 5.2 | 6.0 | 6.2 | 7.6 | 7.4 |
| Periods without TP | 3.9 | 2.9 | 5.3 | 2.3 | 6.2 | 2.5 |

The correlations between predicted and actual changes are in most instances higher for the very near future than for the more distant intervals, though irregularities and contrary cases do not appear uncommon (lines 11–15 and 26–30). If the decline in correlation were actually the rule, this would confirm the presumption that the forecasters do, in one sense, "know more" about the near future (say,

---

[9] For the first subperiod, the error is $(103–100) − (104–100) = −1$; for the second, it is $(104–103) − (108–106) = −1$.

0–3 months) than about the more remote future (say, 12–15 months). It would also give additional support to the hypothesis that it is the bias that accounts mainly for the similarity of typical intraforecast change errors for the different intervals.

### MULTIPERIOD FORECASTS INTERPRETED AS RATE-OF-GROWTH PREDICTIONS

A rough indication that the intraforecast change errors do not generally increase with the distance to the target interval could have been obtained earlier (from Table 9). Reading across that table, one can see that the average errors usually increase less than proportionately to the extension of the span. The errors of twelve-month forecasts are, on the whole, less than twice as large as the errors of six-month forecasts and less than four times as large as those of three-month forecasts. These observations suggest another way of looking at multiperiod forecasts.[10] Suppose that what forecasters really try to do is to predict average rates of growth. Under this assumption, one would want to compute errors by (1) taking differences between the predicted and the actual percentage changes and (2) expressing these differences on a per-unit-of-time basis.[11]

When the mean absolute errors of percentage changes are divided by the length of span, it appears that they become *smaller* the longer the forecast. For example, the figures for the six-month forecasts are 3.14 (percentage points) for set A and 2.38 for set E, while the corresponding figures for the twelve-month forecasts, when divided by two, are 2.81 and 2.06, respectively. The results for quarterly forecast chains also suggest such declines. Thus the figures for set G, obtained by dividing the error measures for spans of one to six quarters by 1, 2, . . . 6, are 1.22, .94, .93, .80, .70, and .60 percentage points.

This may seem puzzling indeed: Are we to infer that the longer forecasts are after all better, not worse, than the very short ones? At this point, it becomes important to consider what the *effective* span of a

[10] I am indebted to Victor Fuchs and Geoffrey Moore of the National Bureau for comments which prompted the approach described here, although they are in no way responsible for the interpretations made.

[11] This amounts to dividing the errors in forecasts of percentage changes by the length of span. Compounding is ignored to simplify matters; given the shortness of the forecasts and our present purpose, this should not be a cause of any significant errors.

forecast is, since the above calculations depend critically on assumptions regarding the relative spans—that, e.g., 0–12 actually represents twice the distance involved in 0–6, etc. But recall that the position at the time "0," that is, on the date of forecast, is itself not known as a rule, but estimated (predicted) with an error.[12] Suppose then that, to account for this, the forecast of the first interval in the chain is treated as if its span were three months longer—0–9 instead of 0–6, for example. The longer forecast, say, 0–12, must be treated accordingly, i.e., as 0–15. In semiannual units, the two spans are no longer to be represented by 1 and 2 but rather by 1.5 and 2.5, and the divisors in our calculations must be changed accordingly.[13]

When the spans are thus recomputed, the following figures are obtained for the mean absolute errors of the implicit forecasts of rates of change: [14]

| Span of Forecast (months) | | GNP (billion dollars): Forecast Sets | | | | Industrial Production (1947–49 = 100): Forecast Sets | | | |
|---|---|---|---|---|---|---|---|---|---|
| "Apparent" | "Effective" | A | E | D | G | A | E | D | G |
| 3 | 6 | | | .48 | .61 | | | .85 | .89 |
| 6 | 9 | 2.09 | 1.59 | .64 | .63 | 2.94 | 2.48 | 1.13 | 1.08 |
| 9 | 12 | | | .49 | .70 | | | .97 | 1.10 |
| 12 | 15 | 2.25 | 1.65 | .43 | .64 | 2.01 | 2.13 | .70 | 1.08 |
| 15 | 18 | | | | .58 | | | | .89 |
| 18 | 21 | | | | .51 | | | | .75 |

These measures show no definite pattern of dependence upon the span of forecast. The adjustment for the fact that the recent past and present must in part also be predicted (because of the lag of information) has removed the previously observed tendency for the mean absolute errors of rate-of-change forecasts to get smaller as the predictions

[12] As shown earlier, subtracting that error algebraically from the error of the level forecast yields the implicit error of predicted change. But this is a matter of defining the latter measure; it does not imply that errors of changes are independent of those of the base (ECP). The following argument assumes dependence between the two error categories in that the imperfection of knowledge about the current position acts as if to lengthen the effective span of forecast.

[13] A similar adjustment for quarterly spans would lead to the use of divisors 2, 3, 4, and 5 (instead of 1, 2, 3, and 4) for the forecasts 0–3, 0–6, 0–9, and 0–12, respectively.

[14] Measures for different forecast sets are not comparable here, not only because of differences in periods covered but also because some of the figures refer to rates per six-month intervals (A,E), while others refer to rates per quarter. The only comparisons intended are those between spans for a given forecast set.

grow longer.[15] The differences between the summary error measures thus obtained are mostly small and irregular. This evidence is consistent with the idea that projection of a certain rate of growth over a sequence of periods often served as a basic device in the construction of these multiperiod forecasts. And this conception fits in, too, with our earlier finding that the intraforecast change errors do not vary systematically with the distance from the present.

To sum up, in this chapter we have developed some tentative and partial explanations of how an increase in the predictive span influences the marginal as well as the average accuracy of forecasts. They include the notions of sustained biases, differentiation between sequences with and without turning points, and modified rate-of-growth projections. These are not competing hypotheses, though they have not yet been integrated. Further evidence and analysis will be necessary to arrive at a more definitive explanation.

### DIRECTIONAL AND TURNING-POINT ERRORS IN MULTIPERIOD FORECASTS

Appraisals of turning-point errors in forecasts of sequences of short intervals present some complications that do not arise in the annual data. In the latter, virtually all turns are associated with business cycle reversals; in series with shorter unit periods, there are some additional directional changes superimposed sporadically on the continuing trend-cycle developments. Such changes often reflect events caused by exogenous forces, which could hardly have been foreseen, and it is at least questionable whether they should be treated on a par with the major cyclical turns.

Also, in the series of short unit periods, runs of negative as well as positive signs occur, i.e., sequences of decreases as well as increases. The corresponding forecast chains can likewise contain runs of either sign. Comparisons of these signs will yield the frequencies of all directional errors, whether or not they are connected with actual or predicted turning points. A distinction can be made here between directional errors and turning-point errors, where the latter represent a subset of

---

[15] In other words, these errors decline with the increase in the "apparent" spans but not with the increase in the "effective" spans (see the tabulation in the text above).

the former. For the annual aggregates, on the other hand, this distinction has virtually no practical significance, since the two categories coincide.[16]

Table 13 presents the frequencies of directional errors for the five sets of multiperiod forecasts of GNP that are used throughout this chapter. These measures refer to the intraforecast changes; comparisons by span are of less interest in this context.[17]

Most of the observed semiannual or quarterly changes in GNP are increases reflecting the trend, though decreases (and, consequently, turning points) are considerably more frequent here than in the annual data, as would be expected. There were relatively few errors of predicting a decline for a period which actually saw a rise in GNP (see columns 2 and 3). Forecasters are, of course, aware of the economy's growth and tend to predict increases most of the time. Indeed, the predominant type of directional error comes about by missing a downturn, that is, predicting a rise for a period in which a decline actually occurred (columns 4 and 5). In two of the sets, all decreases were missed as none at all were predicted (lines 12–19).

The percentages of directional errors are computed by counting all instances of divergent signs of actual and predicted changes and relating the results to the corresponding observation totals. Even though the latter include the large category of actual increases that coincide

[16] Decreases in such series as GNP or industrial production have never lasted as long as two years in the postwar period, nor were they expected to. Only in 1946 and 1947 were declines predicted twice in a row by some forecasters (these would both be classified as "false signals" of peaks).

[17] Scores computed according to the agreement in direction between actual and predicted changes classified by span may be quite sensitive to errors in trend estimation. It is indeed possible (though not likely) that such scores would be poor solely because of misjudgment of the trend. Thus, in the example below, the peak was correctly predicted and dated(*). The intraforecast changes ($\Delta P$) agree in sign with the actual changes ($\Delta A$) in each successive period. Nevertheless, changes predicted for increasing spans, from $t$ to $t + 1$, $t + 2$, etc. (which amount to cumulations of $\Delta P$) disagree in sign with the corresponding actual changes in two of the four intervals.

| | Values of | | Successive Changes | | Changes by Span (cumulated) | |
|---|---|---|---|---|---|---|
| | $P$ | $A$ | $\Delta P$ | $\Delta A$ | Cum $\Delta P$ | Cum $\Delta A$ |
| $t$ | 100 | 100 | | | | |
| $t + 1$ | 103* | 105* | +3 | +5 | +3 | +5 |
| $t + 2$ | 101 | 104 | −2 | −1 | +1 | +4 |
| $t + 3$ | 99 | 102 | −2 | −2 | −1 | +2 |
| $t + 4$ | 98 | 101 | −1 | −1 | −2 | +1 |

## TABLE 13

*Frequency of Directional Errors in Forecasts of*
*Semiannual and Quarterly Changes in GNP,*
*1947-63*

| Line | Interval of Predicted Change (months)[a] | Total Number of Obser- vations (1) | Number of Observed Increases That Were | | Number of Observed Decreases That Were | | Percentage of Directional Errors[b] (6) |
|------|------|------|------|------|------|------|------|
| | | | Predicted (2) | Not Predicted (3) | Predicted (4) | Not Predicted (5) | |
| | | *Forecast Set A: 1947-49, 1955-56, 1958-63* | | | | | |
| 1. | 0-6 | 11 | 7 | 2 | 2 | 0 | 18.2 |
| 2. | 6-12 | 11 | 6 | 2 | 1 | 2 | 36.4 |
| | | *Forecast Set C: 1959-63*[c] | | | | | |
| 3. | 0-3 | 22 | 15 | 4 | 2 | 1 | 22.7 |
| 4. | 3-6 | 20 | 14 | 3 | 1 | 2 | 25.0 |
| 5. | 6-9 | 19[d] | 15 | 1 | 0 | 2 | 16.7 |
| 6. | 9-12 | 13[d] | 10 | 0 | 0 | 2 | 16.7 |
| 7. | 12-15 | 7[d] | 6 | 0 | 0 | 0 | 0 |
| | | *Forecast Set D: 1959-63* | | | | | |
| 8. | 0-3 | 9 | 5 | 1 | 1 | 2 | 33.3 |
| 9. | 3-6 | 9 | 7 | 1 | 0 | 1 | 22.2 |
| 10. | 6-9 | 9 | 6 | 0 | 0 | 3 | 33.3 |
| 11. | 9-12 | 9[d] | 6 | 2 | 0 | 0 | 25.0 |
| | | *Forecast Set E: 1956, 1960-63* | | | | | |
| 12. | 0-6 | 5 | 2 | 3 | 0 | 0 | 60.0 |
| 13. | 6-12 | 5 | 3 | 1 | 0 | 1 | 40.0 |
| | | *Forecast Set G: 1955-63*[e] | | | | | |
| 14. | 0-3 | 16 | 9 | 1 | 0 | 6 | 43.8 |
| 15. | 3-6 | 16 | 13 | 1 | 0 | 2 | 18.8 |
| 16. | 6-9 | 16 | 9 | 1 | 0 | 6 | 43.8 |
| 17. | 9-12 | 16 | 14 | 0 | 0 | 2 | 12.5 |
| 18. | 12-15 | 16 | 10 | 0 | 0 | 6 | 37.5 |
| 19. | 15-18 | 16 | 14 | 0 | 0 | 2 | 12.5 |

*Notes to Table 13*

[a]The current (base) period $t$ is marked 0, so that 0-3 denotes the three-month interval between $t$ and $(t + 3)$; 3-6, the three-month interval between $(t + 3)$ and $(t + 6)$; etc.

[b]Sum of entries in columns 3 and 5, divided by the corresponding entry in line 1 and multiplied by 100. See also note d.

[c]The entries for this set are not strictly comparable because some of the forecast chains are "incomplete," so that the number of observations for different spans varies. See Table 9, note b.

[d]Includes one instance of no change in the actual value matched with a predicted increase; this observation was excluded from the computed percentage of directional errors in column 6.

[e]Based on forecasts in constant prices, as reported.

with predicted increases, the percentages are on the whole large (half of them exceed 25 per cent, see column 6).[18]

To identify directional errors, it is sufficient to compare the signs of actual and predicted changes in any given interval. However, turning points occur when the signs of changes in two successive periods differ; hence, in dealing with errors in forecasting turns, it is necessary to compare *sequences* of signs. A multiperiod forecast may contain directional errors which reflect a previous turning-point error but are not themselves associated with any turning point. It may also contain directional changes which correct previous errors and result in a realignment rather than in a divergence of signs. And it may even contain opposite sequences in the actual and predicted figures, e.g., a "peak" in the former matched by a "trough" in the latter.[19]

[18] Comparisons by span yield similar results here, but, as already noted, they are less appropriate for the study of directional errors than these measures which refer to changes in successive, nonoverlapping intervals.

[19] To illustrate, let the sign sequences be as follows:

| Interval (months) | 0-3 | 3-6 | 6-9 | 9-12 | 12-15 | 15-18 |
|---|---|---|---|---|---|---|
| Sign of actual change | + | + | + | + | − | + |
| Sign of predicted change | + | − | − | + | + | − |

Here there is a turning-point error in the interval 3-6, which is of the "false signal" type. In 6-9, there is a directional error but no new turning-point error. Then the signs of the forecast sequence change again, while those of the actual values do not, but this merely corrects the previous errors and restores the directional agreement between forecasts and realizations (in 9-12). In the interval 12-15, there is another turning-point error, this time of a "missed turn" type. Finally, there is an example of opposite errors in the transition from 12-15 to 15-18: a "trough" in the actual and a "peak" in the predicted values.

To define turning-point errors, they should (a) be associated with changes in sign of either the actual or the predicted change or both, and (b) result in a directional disagreement between the actual and predicted change. This definition excludes (1) the repeated directional error (which does not follow directly upon any sign changes) and (2) the "corrective" directional change (which results in an agreement of signs).[20]

Table 14 presents a count of turning-point errors thus defined (columns 2–6) and, separately, of cases in the two special categories just described (columns 7–9). The errors are classified into "missed turns" and "false signals," as in Table 8. But there is a difficulty with this distinction in the case of opposite turns in predictions and realizations. Such exceptional errors belong, in a sense, to both of these categories and are treated accordingly in Table 14 (see note f). Other decision rules that seemed reasonable were adopted to handle the cases of no change in either actual or predicted values.[21]

The performance of the multiperiod forecasts of GNP in regard to turning points appears to be poor indeed, according to Table 14. The dates of a few turns were correctly predicted, mainly over the shorter spans of three or six months, in three of the forecasts sets. In the more distant intervals, virtually all recorded turns were missed and virtually all predicted turns proved to be false signals. There is little point in presenting the percentages of turns missed and falsely predicted (the $\bar{E}_{T1}$ and $\bar{E}_{T2}$ measures, as in Table 8, columns 8–9); it is enough to observe the predominance of zero entries in the count of the "correctly predicted" turning points (Table 14, column 4). Two of the sets show no correct turning-point forecasts at all (lines 12–19).

Before accepting the verdict implied in these findings, we should point out that our method, in effect, assigns failure marks to all turning-point predictions that did not identify exactly the date of the

[20] It should be noted that (2) can occur in actual as well as predicted sequences. For example, let the signs of the actual changes be + − + and those of the predicted changes + + +. There are two directional changes in the actual values but we count only one turning-point error and assign it to the second interval. The change from the second to the third interval restores the agreement of signs. (See footnote 19 for an example of a "corrective" directional change in the predicted sequence.)

[21] The main rule consists in the distinction between configurations such as + 0 − or − 0 +, which do constitute turning points, and configurations such as + 0 + or − 0 −, which do not.

## TABLE 14

### Frequency of Turning Points and Errors in Forecasts of Semiannual and Quarterly Changes in GNP, 1947-63

| Line | Interval of Predicted Change (months)[a] | Total Number of Observations (1) | Number of Turning Points Counted[b] | | | | | No. of Turning Points Excluded from Count[c] | | Number of Repeated Directional Errors[d] (9) |
|---|---|---|---|---|---|---|---|---|---|---|
| | | | Observed (TT+TN) (2) | Predicted (TT+NT) (3) | Correctly Predicted (TT) (4) | Missed (TN) (5) | Falsely Predicted (NT) (6) | Observed (7) | Predicted (8) | |
| | | | *Forecast Set A: 1947-49, 1955-56, 1958-63* | | | | | | | |
| 1. | 0-6 | 11 | 3 | 4 | 3 | 0 | 1 | 0 | 1 | 0 |
| 2. | 6-12 | 11 | 3 | 2 | 1 | 2 | 1 | 0 | 0 | 1 |
| | | | *Forecast Set C: 1959-63*[e] | | | | | | | |
| 3. | 0-3 | 22 | 4 | 4 | 2 | 2 | 2 | 0 | 1 | 1 |
| 4. | 3-6 | 20 | 4 | 1 | 0 | 4 | 1 | 0 | 5 | 0 |
| 5. | 6-9 | 19 | 3 | 0 | 0 | 3 | 0 | 1 | 3 | 0 |
| 6. | 9-12 | 13 | 2 | 0 | 0 | 2 | 0 | 1 | 1 | 0 |
| 7. | 12-15 | 7 | 0 | 0 | 0 | 0 | 0 | 1 | 0 | 0 |
| | | | *Forecast Set D: 1959-63* | | | | | | | |
| 8. | 0-3 | 9 | 2 | 1 | 0 | 2 | 1 | 0 | 0 | 0 |
| 9. | 3-6 | 9 | 1 | 1 | 1 | 0 | 0 | 1 | 0 | 1 |
| 10. | 6-9 | 9 | 2 | 0 | 0 | 2 | 0 | 0 | 0 | 1 |
| 11. | 9-12 | 9 | 1 | 2 | 0 | 1[f] | 2[f] | 1 | 0 | 0 |

(continued)

## TABLE 14 (concluded)

| Line | Interval of Predicted Change (months)[a] | Total Number of Observations (1) | Number of Turning Points Counted[b] | | | | | No. of Turning Points Excluded from Count[c] | | Number of Repeated Directional Errors[d] (9) |
|---|---|---|---|---|---|---|---|---|---|---|
| | | | Observed (TT+TN) (2) | Predicted (TT+NT) (3) | Correctly Predicted (TT) (4) | Missed (TN) (5) | Falsely Predicted (NT) (6) | Observed (7) | Predicted (8) | |
| | | | *Forecast Set E: 1956, 1960-63* | | | | | | | |
| 12. | 0-6 | 5 | 0 | 0 | 0 | 0 | 0 | 1 | 0 | 0 |
| 13. | 6-12 | 5 | 1 | 1 | 0 | 1 | 1 | 0 | 0 | 0 |
| | | | *Forecast Set G: 1955-63[g]* | | | | | | | |
| 14. | 0-3 | 16 | 4 | 1 | 0 | 4[f] | 1[f] | 0 | 1 | 2 |
| 15. | 3-6 | 16 | 0 | 1 | 0 | 0 | 1 | 2 | 0 | 2 |
| 16. | 6-9 | 16 | 4 | 0 | 0 | 4 | 0 | 0 | 0 | 3 |
| 17. | 9-12 | 16 | 0 | 0 | 0 | 0 | 0 | 3 | 1 | 2 |
| 18. | 12-15 | 16 | 4 | 0 | 0 | 4 | 0 | 0 | 0 | 2 |
| 19. | 15-18 | 16 | 1 | 0 | 0 | 1 | 0 | 2 | 0 | 1 |

[a]The base period $t$ is marked 0, so that 0-3 denotes the three-month interval between $t$ and $(t+3)$, etc. The table covers the same forecast sets as previous tables in this chapter.

[b]Excludes the directional changes listed in columns 7 and 8. For symbols used, see text above.

[c]Directional changes that correct previous turning-point errors and result in agreement of signs of actual and predicted changes. See text and footnotes 19 and 20.

[d]Includes instances of divergent signs which have not changed from the preceding period. See text and footnote 19.

[e]The entries for this set are not strictly comparable because of differences in the number of available observations. See Table 9, note b.

[f]Includes one instance of opposite sequences of signs in the actual and predicted figures. See text and footnote 19.

[g]Based on forecasts in constant prices, as reported.

event. Now the objection could be raised that the requirement of exact dating of turning points in the chained (multiperiod) forecasts is too demanding. Moreover, some of the recorded directional changes have been short and shallow; in fact, some would be reversed by later data revisions. Failure to foresee such movements should not be considered a significant error, and in fact smoothing them out could under some circumstances be desirable.

The latter argument has a certain validity. Some of the directional changes involved were in fact reversed in the following quarter, and the agreement in sign of actual and predicted changes was often restored as promptly. An indication of this is provided where the "corrective" changes are frequent and the repeated directional errors rare (as in set C, lines 3–7, columns 7–9). Elsewhere, however, more sustained errors are in evidence (see, in particular, the high frequencies of repeated errors in lines 14–19, column 9). One can hardly dismiss all the errors recorded in Tables 13 and 14 on the ground that the changes to which they refer were all short and small.[22]

Recognizing that errors of misdating should not be judged too severely,[23] we have examined the importance of such errors by treating each multiperiod forecast as a single pattern and waiving the requirement of exact dating. For example, if a four-quarter chain forecast featured a rise followed by a decline (say, $+ + - -$), and a peak did actually occur within the next twelve months but sooner than foreseen ($+ - - -$), then the forecast would be considered a correct prediction of that peak.

The outcome of this analysis can be simply stated: misdating was relatively unimportant as a source of errors in the forecasts under discussion. What happened in the great majority of turning-point errors was that the forecaster either (1) predicted a continuous development and missed a reversal, or (2) predicted a reversal which did not occur. In fact, despite the relaxation of the requirement of exact dating, com-

---

[22] A direct, detailed examination of the differences among the movements involved should be rewarding when richer materials become available, but it is not required to bear out the above statement.

[23] Suppose that a forecaster correctly predicted that a turn would occur the following year but misdated the turn by one quarter. This might be no mean achievement under the circumstances, yet one of the four interquarter changes in the given year would be marked wrong, yielding an error score of 25 per cent.

parisons of the sign patterns need not be more favorable to forecasters than the measures given in Tables 13 and 14.[24]

If the periods covered by the successive chain forecasts overlap, as in the case of forecasts C, D, and G, which are issued twice or four times in a year, the same error can reappear and be counted more than once. Again, however, this factor does not alter our main conclusion, which can now be stated with considerable assurance. Despite the possible mitigating circumstances that were considered, the record, whichever way one looks at it, simply does *not* indicate any significant ability of forecasters to predict a turning point several months ahead.[25]

### SECTORAL FORECASTS FOR DIFFERENT SPANS

Forecasts of GNP components in set C were analyzed for spans varying from three to fifteen months. The results, based on chain predictions made in each quarter between 1958 and 1963, are summarized in Table 15.

This table demonstrates the pervasive tendency of errors to increase with the length of the forecast. There are only a few, rather slight exceptions to the rule that the mean absolute errors or the root mean square errors grow steadily larger as the predictions reach further into the future. Evidently, the rule applies to variables with very different characteristics.

Again, as in Table 9 for GNP and industrial production, the errors in Table 15 increase less than proportionately to the indicated length of span. If the entries in column 2 were divided by two, those in column 3 by three, etc., the errors thus computed in the rates of change

---

[24] This is so because the measures given in Table 13 assign a common error to the chain forecast as a whole, whereas those in Table 14 result in many separate scores, one for each different future interval, and usually only some of these scores will reflect the error. In fact, comparing the sign patterns often yields results that are particularly, and sometimes unfairly, negative. The following are some of the results for the GNP forecasts (recall that $N$ denotes the absence and $T$ the presence of a turning point; the first symbol refers to the actual and the second to the predicted values).

| Forecast Set | No. of Chain Forecasts | NN | TT | TN | NT | Opposite Turns in $P_t$ and $A_t$ |
|---|---|---|---|---|---|---|
| A | 11 | 5 | 2 | 2 | 2 | |
| D | 9 | 2 | 1 | 3 | 2 | 1 |
| G | 16 | 4 | | 11 | 1 | |

[25] A parallel study of the record of industrial production forecasts also leads to this conclusion.

TABLE 15

*Forecasts of Eight Selected Components of GNP: Summary Measures of Error over Spans from Three to Fifteen Months, 1958-63*[a]

| Line | Predicted Variable | Span of Forecast (months) | | | | |
|---|---|---|---|---|---|---|
| | | Three (1) | Six (2) | Nine (3) | Twelve (4) | Fifteen (5) |
| | | *Mean Absolute Errors (percentage points)* | | | | |
| 1. | Personal consumption expenditures | 0.62 | 0.95 | 1.24 | 1.50 | 1.82 |
| 2. | Consumer durables | 4.03 | 4.44 | 4.45 | 5.03 | 7.83 |
| 3. | Gross private domestic investment | 4.75 | 9.42 | 9.69 | 10.76 | 14.23 |
| 4. | Plant and equipment outlays | 2.40 | 3.77 | 5.21 | 6.75 | 9.13 |
| 5. | Residential construction | 4.20 | 6.64 | 6.52 | 5.91 | 5.53 |
| 6. | Government expenditures | 1.15 | 1.41 | 1.68 | 2.24 | 2.37 |
| | | *Mean Absolute Errors (billion dollars)* | | | | |
| 7. | Net change in inventories | 2.14 | 4.38 | 4.35 | 5.14 | 5.44 |
| 8. | Net foreign balance | 0.91 | 1.18 | 1.07 | 1.24 | 1.46 |
| | | *Mean Errors (percentage points)* | | | | |
| 9. | Personal consumption expenditures | −0.30 | −0.41 | −0.46 | −0.53 | −1.10 |
| 10. | Consumer durables | −1.55 | −0.52 | −1.20 | −0.38 | −4.99 |
| 11. | Gross private domestic investment | −0.32 | −1.92 | −2.61 | −1.76 | −7.73 |
| 12. | Plant and equipment outlays | 0.07 | −1.23 | −3.13 | −3.50 | −6.04 |
| 13. | Residential construction | 0.24 | −1.89 | −4.06 | −4.29 | −5.08 |
| 14. | Government expenditures | −0.26 | −0.53 | −0.85 | −1.49 | −1.58 |
| | | *Mean Errors (billion dollars)* | | | | |
| 15. | Net change in inventories | −0.40 | −0.14 | 0.90 | 1.52 | −1.07 |
| 16. | Net foreign balance | −0.22 | −0.31 | −0.51 | −0.46 | −1.46 |

[a]For consumer durables (lines 2 and 10), forecasts cover the period 1961-63. The numbers of observations for spans of 3 to 15 months are 13, 11, 10, 7, and 4. For net foreign balance (lines 8 and 16), forecasts cover the period 1958-63. The numbers of observations for spans of 3 to 15 months are 19, 17, 16, 10, and 5. For the remainder, forecasts also cover the period 1958-63. The numbers of observations are 21, 20, 19, 13, and 7 for spans of 3, 6, 9, 12, and 15 months, respectively. The numbers vary because some of the forecast chains do not include all spans (see Table 9, note b).

would systematically and strongly decrease. But, as pointed out before, this procedure is incorrect inasmuch as it disregards the fact that fore-casters must in effect predict a little backward in time as well as for-ward. When, to make a broad allowance for this, each span is treated as if it were one quarter longer (that is, each divisor is increased by one; see pages 5–18 above), the resulting mean absolute errors of rates of change (in percentage points) show much smaller and more irregu-lar differences, though they still tend to decline with the span in some cases.[26]

| | Effective Span of Forecast (months) | | | | |
| --- | --- | --- | --- | --- | --- |
| | Six | Nine | Twelve | Fifteen | Eighteen |
| Pers. consumption expenditures | 0.31 | 0.32 | 0.31 | 0.30 | 0.31 |
| Consumer durables | 2.02 | 1.48 | 1.11 | 1.01 | 1.30 |
| Gross priv. dom. investment | 2.37 | 3.14 | 2.42 | 2.15 | 2.37 |
| Plant and equipm. expenditures | 1.20 | 1.25 | 1.30 | 1.35 | 1.52 |
| Resid. construction | 2.10 | 2.21 | 1.63 | 1.18 | 0.92 |
| Government expenditures | 0.58 | 0.47 | 0.42 | 0.45 | 0.40 |

The mean arithmetic errors are again found to be predominantly negative (Table 15, lines 9–16). They also tend to increase absolutely with the span of the forecasts, though this association is considerably less regular than the others.

[26] The "effective" span of forecast is obtained by adding 3 to the "apparent" span (listed in Table 15). The following figures for mean absolute errors of rates of change (in percentage points) illustrate the results of using the divisors for the apparent rather than those for the effective spans:

| | Apparent Span of Forecast (months) | | | | |
| --- | --- | --- | --- | --- | --- |
| | Three | Six | Nine | Twelve | Fifteen |
| Pers. consumption expenditures | 0.62 | 0.48 | 0.41 | 0.38 | 0.36 |
| Consumer durables | 4.03 | 2.22 | 1.48 | 1.26 | 1.57 |
| Gross private dom. investment | 4.75 | 4.71 | 3.23 | 2.69 | 2.85 |
| Government expenditures | 1.15 | 0.70 | 0.56 | 0.56 | 0.47 |

# 6

# YARDSTICKS OF PREDICTIVE
# PERFORMANCE

### EXTRAPOLATIVE MODELS

The average error measures show how much the forecasts deviate from the unattainable ideal of no error. More realistic criteria are necessary to take account of the properties of the variables being forecast and the degree of difficulty they present to the forecaster.

The past record of the series to be predicted contains information that may have predictive value and should be exploited by the forecaster. To make use of it, some mechanical procedure is needed to extrapolate the past; since no other variables are employed, there is no place here for a theory of what economic factors determine the variable being predicted or how they operate. In this sense of being innocent of economic theory proper, all extrapolations are "naive" models (as they have been called) including some that are technically rather sophisticated.

The simplest extrapolative models, which have long been in use for this purpose, are indeed naive. The first of these (N1) predicts that the next period's value of a given variable will equal this period's value; another (N2) projects forward the last recorded change in a series, thus replacing the "same level" assumption of the first model with a "same change" assumption.[1]

Clearly, naive models of this kind should be regarded merely as providing minimal standards, which may be useful for screening out poor forecasts but are not sufficient to rate the surviving forecasts as neces-

---

[1] N1 can be said to specify that $A_{t+1} = A_t + u_{t+1}$, where $u$ is a random error. Hence the forecast here is $P_{N1} = A_t^*$ (the preliminary estimate of the current value of the series). N2 specifies that $A_{t+1} = A_t + \Delta A_t + u_{t+1}$, and the corresponding forecast is $P_{N2} = A_t^* + \Delta A_t^*$.

sarily good. The ideal extrapolation would be the one which takes best advantage of the historical content of the series for the predictive purpose, that is, the one that in the long run yields smaller errors than any other extrapolation. Then, a comparison of a forecast proper with such an extrapolation would show whether the forecaster's judgment or knowledge of the relevant economic relations gives better results than those obtained through the optimum use of the predicted variable's own record.[2]

To achieve the optimum extrapolation, a sufficiently long and consistent time series record for a given variable and a knowledge of its structure are necessary. At best, it might be possible to move closer to that ideal goal by constructing improved extrapolative models with the aid of trend projections, autoregressive schemes, and other devices.[3]

In one such approach, we use a simple but frequently rather effective type of extrapolation, which adds the average value of past changes in the series to the latest level of the series. This model, called N2*, is a projection of the mean historical change, an extension of model N2, which projects merely the last recorded change. For series with pronounced trends which are approximately linear over the periods covered, model N2* has a considerable advantage.[4]

Another approach uses an autoregressive model (N3), in which the present level is taken as a linear function of the preceding levels of the series, plus a random error.[5] This method imposes greater requirements on the data than the other, simpler models. The relationships between present and past values cannot be measured with reasonable confidence for any single series as short as those used here. Only very simple relations can be detected within such series. Obtaining large

---

[2] Jacob Mincer developed a method of comparing a forecast with an extrapolation which in effect decomposes them both into their common elements and their separate predictive contributions. A paper on the criteria of forecast evaluation by Mincer and myself, "The Evaluation of Economic Forecasts," will include a description and illustration of that method.

[3] Work in this area is continuing. See the reports by Jon Cunnyngham in the National Bureau Annual Reports for 1964 and 1965.

[4] The assumption of N2* is that $A_{t+1} = A_t + \overline{\Delta A} + u_{t+1}$, where $\overline{\Delta A}$ is the average value of past changes in the given series as available to the forecaster from the historical record. Hence, the forecast $P_{N2}{}^* = A_t{}^* + \overline{\Delta A}$.

[5] The general form of N3 is $A_{t+1} = a + b_1 A_t + b_2 A_{t-1} + b_3 A_{t-2} + \cdots u_{t+1}$. The forecast uses estimates of $a$ and $b$'s from regressions based on the values of $A$ as available in the base period $t$ (these are typically preliminary, $A_1{}^*$ at least for $t$). The value $u_{t+1}$ is assumed zero.

numbers of usable observations for the variables concerned is, however, also very difficult.[6]

The extrapolative models have been developed in quarterly terms in order to appraise the chained forecasts with varying spans, to allow for the timing of the forecasts, and to realize any possible gains from the additional information conveyed by quarterly data. The annual bench-mark forecasts were computed by averaging the extrapolations for the four quarters of a given year. Much has been learned through work in this area about how extrapolations of different types are related to the predictive span, quality of the data, variability of the series, etc. These lessons are pertinent for the appraisal of forecasts proper, inasmuch as the latter contain elements of extrapolation, and I shall refer to them repeatedly in this chapter.

Many economic time series, and particularly comprehensive aggre-gates such as GNP, are highly autocorrelated. This implies high cor-relations among the lagged terms in the N3 equations. The large standard errors of all but a very few of the regression coefficients of these terms reflect the resulting multicollinearity. In quarterly regres-sions only the two shortest lags appeared significant according to the $t$-tests of these coefficients. Even tests of the combined significance of several additional terms taken together would not give any definite support for inclusion of earlier terms (longer lags) in the N3 regres-sion.[7] Nevertheless experiments showed that addition of a few longer lags does, on the whole, improve the accuracy of the extrapolations. The $R_3$ ratios for GNP and industrial production presented in the next section are based on autoregressive equations with five lagged terms $(A_{t-i}, i = 1, 2, \ldots 5)$.

This illustrates the basic difficulty of inferring predictive properties

---

[6] Quarterly figures for GNP and components in the period before World War II are of questionable quality. The use of wartime data raises serious problems that are familiar. Apart from the quality and consistency of the data, there is the basic question of the continuity of the process or processes they measure. The issue here is over what period a sufficiently stable autoregressive structure can be assumed.

[7] These tests used $F$-ratios of the general form $\dfrac{1 - \bar{R}^2_{t,\, t-1,\, \ldots\, t-k}}{1 - \bar{R}^2_{t,\, t-1,\, \ldots\, t-n}}$, where $k < n$, to determine the past period $A_{t-k}$ for which the additional set $A_{t-k-1}$ to $A_n$ yields no further increase in $\bar{R}^2$ (the adjusted multiple determination coefficient for the autoregressive equation N3). The results noted in the text were obtained even on standards regarded conventionally as "loose," such as significance levels of .10 and above.

from statistical estimates obtained from historical data. Regression statistics, for example, may often do little more than describe some average relations within the period of fit. Such information is likely to prove insufficient for developing decision rules to guide the forecaster (e.g., rules on how many and which lagged terms to include in a predictive autoregressive model).

This paper relies mainly on N1 and N2*, the last level and the average change extrapolations introduced in Table 1. Model N2 gives inferior results for most of the variables examined. Work with autoregressive models such as N3 yields worthwhile information about the properties of both the time series data and extrapolative predictions, but it still poses serious problems of principle and application.

### ANNUAL FORECASTS VS. EXTRAPOLATIONS

Comparisons of forecasts proper with benchmark forecasts derived from the extrapolative models were made by calculating the ratios of the corresponding root mean square errors $(M_P/M_N)$. As noted in the section on bias in Chapter 4, these measures involve squaring the individual forecast errors, which results in greater weights being attached to larger than to smaller deviations from the recorded values.[8] The ratios bear the subscript of the model used in computing the denominator, e.g., $R_1 = M_P/M_{N1}$. Accordingly our four models provide as many ratios: $R_1$, $R_2$, $R_2$*, and $R_3$.

For annual forecasts of GNP and industrial production, comparisons with all four models are presented. The root mean square errors of the extrapolations for the period 1953–63 are as follows:

|  | $M_{N1}$ | $M_{N2}$ | $M_{N2}$* | $M_{N3}$ |
|---|---|---|---|---|
| GNP (billion dollars) | 24.60 | 19.34 | 15.31 | 15.39 |
| Industrial production (1947–49 = 100) | 10.58 | 11.78 | 9.91 | 9.61 |

Table 16 shows that, for the annual forecasts of GNP and industrial production, the ratios generally are less than unity, indicating that these predictions pass the extrapolative model tests (i.e., $M_P < M_N$).

---

[8] That is, $M^2{}_P = \dfrac{1}{n}\Sigma(P_t - A_t)^2$. More nearly comparable with the other summary measures of predictive accuracy (the simple arithmetic and absolute averages) is the square root of the above figure, $M_P$. Except in the trivial case where all errors are equal, $M_P$ is always larger than the mean absolute error $|\bar{E}|$ (and the latter is larger than the mean error $\bar{E}$).

# TABLE 16

## Annual Forecasts of GNP and Industrial Production: Comparisons with Four Extrapolative Models, 1953-63

| Line | Forecast Set[a] | Period Covered | Root Mean Square Error,[b] $M_P$ (1) | $R_1$ (2) | $R_2$ (3) | $R_2^*$ (4) | $R_3$ (5) |
|------|------|------|------|------|------|------|------|
| | | | | Root Mean Square Errors: Ratios of Forecast to Extrapolation[c] | | | |
| | | | *Gross National Product* | | | | |
| 1. | A | 1954-63 | 12.51 | .506 | .651 | .781 | .798 |
| 2. | B | 1953-63 | 10.69 | .435 | .553 | .699 | .695 |
| 3. | C | 1958-63 | 11.04 | .424 | .534 | .797 | .686 |
| 4. | D | 1956-63 | 11.40 | .459 | .631 | .939 | .758 |
| 5. | E | 1953-63 | 16.71 | .679 | .864 | 1.091 | 1.086 |
| 6. | F | 1953-63 | 8.84 | .359 | .457 | .578 | .574 |
| 7. | G | 1953-63 | 7.93 | .322 | .410 | .518 | .515 |
| 8. | H | 1954-63 | 12.05 | .487 | .626 | .752 | .768 |
| | | | *Industrial Production* | | | | |
| 9. | A | 1954-63 | 5.76 | .559 | .491 | .554 | .618 |
| 10. | C | 1958-63 | 4.92 | .515 | .393 | .582 | .453 |
| 11. | D | 1954-63 | 5.28 | .512 | .450 | .508 | .566 |
| 12. | E | 1954-63 | 5.78 | .561 | .493 | .556 | .620 |
| 13. | F | 1953-63 | 4.65 | .440 | .395 | .469 | .484 |
| 14. | G | 1953-63 | 4.83 | .457 | .410 | .487 | .503 |
| 15. | H | 1954-63 | 4.68 | .454 | .399 | .450 | .502 |

[a]This table covers the same forecast sets as Table 1. It refers to forecasts of levels only. For details, see notes to Table 1.

[b]The general formula for the root mean square error is $M_P = \sqrt{\frac{1}{n} \sum (P-A)^2}$, where $P$ and $A$ are forecasts and actual values, respectively, and the summation is over the periods covered by the forecasts (see text and footnote 7). Entries in this column are in billion dollars for GNP (lines 1-8) and in index points (1947-49 = 100) for industrial production (lines 9-15).

[c]The ratios are: $R_1 = M_P/M_{N1}$; $R_2 = M_P/M_{N2}$; $R_2^* = M_P/M_{N2}^*$; and $R_3 = M_P/M_{N3}$. The denominators, $M_N$, are the root mean square errors of four types of extrapolations. N1 refers to the projection of the last known level, N2 to that of the last known change, N2* to that of the average historical change, and N3 to that of the average relation between the present value of the series and its past values (based on regressions of $A_1$ on $A_{t-i}$, $i = 1, 2, \ldots 5$). See text for more detail.

The measures refer to level forecasts, but the corresponding ratios for change forecasts are similar and the statement applies to them as well.[9]

For GNP, the $R_3$ ratios are about equal to $R_2*$ in the periods after 1953–54, and considerably lower in the years after 1956 or 1958. The $R_2$ ratios are substantially smaller and $R_1$ still lower. This means that N3 or N2* provide the most stringent standards and N1 the easiest. Judging solely from these measures, forecasters in one group would not have done much worse if they had simply extrapolated the recent trend in the manner of N2*, and in another case such extrapolation would have actually done better (lines 4 and 5).

However, it should be recalled that the changes predicted from year to year by forecasters are generally well correlated with the actual changes (see Charts 1 and 2 and text in Chapter 3). As will be shown in the following section (Chart 3 and text), changes derived by extrapolations show much lower correlations with the recorded changes. This advantage of greater efficiency (higher correlations with $\Delta A$) is not necessarily offset by the disadvantage of greater bias that the forecasts usually have relative to such extrapolations as N2* and N3. While these aspects of forecasters' performance are important, they cannot be revealed by the root mean square errors $M$, which measure the over-all accuracy of predictions as affected by both bias and efficiency. To deal with the two aspects separately, it is necessary to compare other measures than just the total $M$ figures.

For industrial production, the simplest extrapolations (N1) would have done surprisingly well recently. In fact, the $R_1$ ratios here are throughout higher than $R_2$, about equal to $R_2*$ in the period after 1953–54, and only moderately lower than $R_3$ (Table 16, lines 9, 11–15). In the latter part of the period covered, $R_1$ was exceeded only by $R_2*$ (line 10).

Comparisons in terms of index numbers on a common base showed the mean absolute errors to be, as a rule, somewhat larger for the industrial production forecasts than for the corresponding GNP forecasts (Table 1, lines 9–22, columns 4 and 5). However, the $M_P/M_N$

---

[9] The ratios are more meaningful for the levels, since the forecasters' base estimates (ECP) are themselves often derived by, or attributed to, some kind of extrapolation. Where the errors with respect to the base values are smaller for the forecasts than for the extrapolations, the level ratios will typically be more favorable to the forecasts than the change ratios. This is true for the cases mentioned earlier in which the ECP errors make the predictions of levels more inaccurate than those of changes.

ratios in Table 16 tend to be lower for industrial production than for GNP, when compared for the same sources and extrapolative models. This would suggest that, relative to these extrapolations, industrial production was predicted better than GNP. But it is important to note that this result depends on the particular extrapolative procedures adopted. To make the measures for the two variables and for the different models comparable, the models were computed in all cases on the assumption that the last value known to the forecaster is that for the third quarter of the base year. This fits well enough the situation for GNP, a quarterly series, but industrial production is available monthly and those who forecast this variable at the end of the year usually know its preliminary estimate for October and may even know that for November. When models N1, N2, and N2* for industrial production were recomputed, with November as the last known position or base, very considerable improvements of the extrapolations and corresponding increases in the $R$ ratios were obtained, compared with the results shown in Table 16, lines 9–15.[10]

The differences between the extrapolations for GNP and industrial production reflect differences in the behavior of the two series over time. To take the simplest illustration, it is clear that N1 yields smaller errors than N2 at turning points. In general, N1 performs better on the more cyclical and irregular series. N2 performs better only for smooth series with persistent trends. Industrial production fluctuated considerably more than GNP; its growth was somewhat weaker and less steady. This can explain why N2 is better than N1 for the annual predictions of GNP but worse for industrial production.

Again, it is instructive to compare N1 and N2* in this context. The main weakness of the former model is that, in disregarding change, it produces forecasts with a large bias (underestimation errors for the growing series). Model N2* corrects largely for this bias, but it too is worse than N1 on turning points (and also on marked retar-

[10] The $R_1$ ratios showed the greatest increases, of up to 50 per cent; on the November base, these ratios fall in the .65 to .80 range and considerably exceed the corresponding measures for GNP. The increases in $R_2$* ratios were much smaller and those in $R_2$ still smaller (note that the weight of the base period is smaller in models N2 and N2* than in N1). Among the recomputed ratios, $R_1$ exceeded the others, except in the most recent years when the $R_2$* ratios were higher (the $R_3$ ratios were not recomputed; our autoregressive extrapolations all use quarterly data only).

dations). As already indicated, the role of the bias is greater for GNP, and that of the turning-point errors for industrial production.[11]

PATTERNS OF ERRORS IN FORECASTS AND EXTRAPOLATIONS

Chart 5 shows for benchmark extrapolations what Charts 1 and 2 showed for the forecasts proper. It is clear that the results for the extrapolations are decidedly inferior.

Consider the model N2*, that is, the projections of average histori- cal change, which turned out to be relatively effective for GNP in terms of the over-all average errors (Table 16). Chart 5 shows that the changes predicted by this model are nearly constant from one year to the next; they approximate a straight line cutting through the "ac- tual" GNP changes at the $20 billion level. This, of course, would be necessarily so for any series with a pronounced and relatively stable growth rate, and the results for industrial production are indeed very similar to those for GNP.

In short, the strength of N2* lies in its being a relatively good trend estimate, thus nearly free of bias. But the weakness of this model lies in its being poorly correlated with the actual changes (in other words, in the high residual variance component of its errors). Espe- cially in periods of large deviations from the trend, as in the recession years 1954 and 1958, the errors produced by N2* must be and obvi- ously are large, as shown in Chart 5, for both GNP and industrial pro- duction.

The autoregressive model N3, which uses lags of one to five quarters, yields forecasts that, unlike those of N2*, vary a great deal from year to year. However, the correlation of these forecasts with actual changes is low for GNP and only moderate (though significant) for industrial production. The errors of the two models are similar in size. They also show some correspondence in their year-to-year changes, notably peak values in the 1953–54 and 1957–58 intervals.

Thus it is easy to see that, in terms of correlation with actual

[11] Further evidence along the same lines is provided by results for other variables. Consumption is similar to GNP in smoothness and trend, and for both series the models N2* and N3 rank highest and N1 the lowest. (Five lagged terms are needed in both cases to make N3 about as good as N2*.) For plant and equipment expendi- tures, a series with more variability and less trend than the others, N3 turns out to be the best of the models within the whole range of one to five lagged terms. Here, as for the production index, N1 ranks higher than N2*, and N2 is the worst.

## CHART 5

*Two Types of Extrapolations of Industrial Production and GNP,*
*Actual and Predicted Changes and Errors, 1953–63*

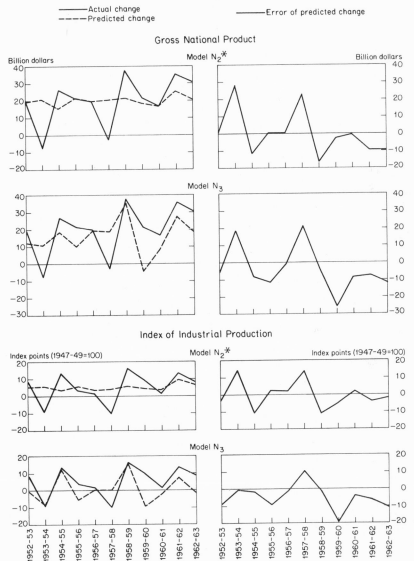

————Actual change
– – – –Predicted change

————Error of predicted change

Gross National Product

Model $N_2$*

Index of Industrial Production

Model $N_2$*

Model $N_3$

changes, the annual forecasts of GNP and industrial production are definitely better than either of the extrapolations N2* and N3. The coefficients of correlation between actual and predicted changes in the tabulation below for 1953–63 provide numerical evidence in support of this statement:

|  | Forecasts | | | Extrapolations | |
| --- | --- | --- | --- | --- | --- |
|  | E | F | G | N2* | N3 |
| GNP | .642 | .900 | .882 | .182 | .424 |
| Industrial production | .753 | .920 | .895 | .535 | .601 |

The fact that the actual and predicted year-to-year changes in GNP and industrial production are in general well correlated should not be interpreted to mean that the changes are effectively forecast a full year ahead. Our analysis of the multiperiod forecasts shows that forecasters typically achieve a considerable measure of success in predicting the next one or two quarters ahead, but limited success beyond that. Let us also recall that the annual record can likewise be interpreted as implying an effective forecasting range of little more than two quarters. Not only are the forecasts typically made late in the preceding calendar year, but patterns of performance very similar to those shown here could be obtained merely by accurately forecasting the first one or two quarters of the ensuing year and assuming no change beyond that. This is indicated by our experiments with *ex-post* extrapolations summarized later in this chapter (see Table 19 and Chart 5).

### SECTORAL FORECASTS, EXTRAPOLATIONS, AND BUSINESSMEN'S ANTICIPATIONS

The summary measures of relative error show forecasts of consumption to be better than forecasts of government spending and much better than those of investment (Table 5, column 1). When taken relative to the extrapolative benchmark models, however, consumption often comes out *worse* than either investment or government expenditures (Table 17, columns 2 and 3). In fact, the $R_2$* ratios in set F exceed unity only for consumption and residential construction. They are very high for all three of the major consumption components, which indicates the marked inferiority of these forecasts to simple trend extrapolations. Consumption of durables, which is by far the most variable of these components and which has the largest errors of relative change, shows the lowest $R_2$* ratio of the three. The corresponding ratios for consumption forecasts B and C are only slightly less than one.

Since consumption has been rising steadily in recent years, the strong showing of the trend extrapolation produced by the N2* model is not difficult to understand. This applies particularly to consumption of nondurables and services. Other GNP components are much less smooth, hence for them such projections are far less effective.

It is clear that the consumption forecasts fail to make use of much information in the past behavior of households that could have significantly improved the forecasts. Consumption may be able to provide the greatest *scope* for improvement of the GNP expenditure forecasts.

Forecasts of construction (especially residential), changes in inventories, and net foreign investment are greatly in need of improvement. Although these series have relatively weak trends and strong cyclical and irregular variations, the N2* extrapolations for them are often nearly as good as the forecasts proper, and sometimes better. This finding will be recognized as particularly unfavorable to the forecasts, since the extrapolations must be rather inefficient here (unlike the case of consumption). The evidence on construction is given in Table 17. The forecasts of net changes in inventories and net foreign investment, as can be seen from the tabulation below, tend to be weak and inferior to the total investment forecasts (the ratios are particularly high for the A forecasts which, it must be remembered, have considerably longer spans than the others). Since these variables assume negative values, the ratios shown are based on absolute change errors.[12]

| | $R_2$* Ratios for Forecast Sets | | |
| --- | --- | --- | --- |
| | A | B | F |
| Gross private domestic investment | 1.360 | .883 | .618 |
| Net change in inventories | 1.457 | 1.048 | .843 |
| Net foreign investment | 1.185 | 1.017 | .992 |

Forecasts of producers' durable equipment are in most cases better relative to extrapolations than forecasts of consumption, housing, inventory changes, and net foreign investment. The same is true of the forecasts of total plant and equipment outlays, although the record for the plant (or nonresidential construction) component tends to be worse

---

[12] The differences between the ratios for absolute and those for percentage errors tend to be small when both units of measurement are applicable (compare the ratios for GPDI in the above tabulation and in Table 17).

TABLE 17

*Forecasts of Relative Changes in Major Components of GNP:*
*Comparisons with Extrapolative Models, 1953-63*

| Line | Predicted Variable | Root Mean Square Error, $M_P$ (percentage points) (1) | Root Mean Square Errors: Ratio of Forecast to Extrapolation $R_1$ (2) | $R_2^*$ (3) |
|---|---|---|---|---|
| | | *Forecast Set B: 1953-63* | | |
| 1. | Gross national product | 2.15 | .395 | .660 |
| 2. | Personal consumption expenditures | 1.52 | .318 | .911 |
| 3. | Gross private domestic investment | 12.83 | .901 | 1.010 |
| 4. | Plant and equipment | 7.80 | .901 | 1.127 |
| 5. | Housing | 14.12 | 1.229 | 2.028 |
| 6. | Total government expenditures: | 2.82 | .406 | .457 |
| 7. | Federal | 5.48 | .681 | .605 |
| 8. | State and local | 2.01 | .239 | 1.214 |
| | | *Forecast Set F: 1953-63* | | |
| 9. | Gross national product | 1.70 | .312 | .521 |
| 10. | Personal consumption expenditures | 1.69 | .354 | 1.015 |
| 11. | Gross private domestic investment | 7.20 | .506 | .567 |
| 12. | Total government expenditures | 2.15 | .309 | .348 |
| | | *Forecast Set F: Other Periods* [a] | | |
| 13. | Consumer durables | 5.36 | .663 | 1.250 |
| 14. | Consumer nondurables | 1.56 | .444 | 2.425 |
| 15. | Consumer services | 1.78 | .280 | 1.334 |
| 16. | Producers' durables | 6.05 | .495 | .603 |
| 17. | Nonresidential construction | 4.01 | .719 | .904 |
| 18. | Residential nonfarm construction | 9.15 | .931 | 1.596 |
| 19. | Federal government expenditures | 1.86 | .315 | .527 |
| 20. | State and local expenditures | 1.35 | .160 | .741 |

*(continued)*

TABLE 17 *(concluded)*

| Line | Predicted Variable | Root Mean Square Error, $M_P$ (percentage points) (1) | Root Mean Square Errors: Ratio of Forecast to Extrapolation | |
|------|-------------------|:---:|:---:|:---:|
| | | | $R_1$ (2) | $R_2*$ (3) |
| | | *Forecast Set A: 1958-63* | | |
| 21. | Gross national product | 1.92 | .368 | 1.027 |
| 22. | Personal consumption expenditures | 1.01 | .222 | .771 |
| 23. | Consumer durables | 5.21 | .901 | .935 |
| 24. | Gross private domestic investment | 11.43 | 1.118 | 1.255 |
| 25. | Producers' durables | 6.36 | .562 | .593 |
| 26. | New construction | 5.08 | .898 | 1.917 |
| 27. | Total government expenditures | 3.15 | .410 | .861 |
| | | *Forecast Set C: 1958-63* | | |
| 28. | Gross national product | 2.04 | .374 | .726 |
| 29. | Personal consumption expenditures | 1.44 | .310 | .960 |
| 30. | Gross private domestic investment | 8.50 | .570 | .666 |
| 31. | Plant and equipment | 4.95 | .597 | .643 |
| 32. | Residential construction | 9.04 | .865 | 2.251 |
| 33. | Total government expenditures | 2.17 | .319 | .893 |
| 34. | Federal | 3.56 | .593 | 1.027 |
| 35. | State and local | 1.94 | .232 | 1.019 |

[a]Entries on lines 13-15 cover 1959-63; lines 16, 19, and 20, 1955-63; lines 17 and 18, 1956-63.

Note: This table covers the same forecast sets as Table 5 and, like the latter, uses measures based on errors of percentage changes (as defined in Chapter 4, text and note 5). The extrapolations match the forecasts strictly (for set A, they refer to the last quarter of the year wherever the forecasts do, see Table 5, note c; in all other cases, they are annual).

than that for equipment.[13] A marked exception, however, is provided by set B, in which the plant and equipment predictions are decidedly poor, worse than the trend projections and than the predictions for all but two GNP components (see Table 17, column 3).

[13] Compare lines 16 and 17, columns 2 and 3, of Table 17. It should be noted that the opposite is true of the absolute errors; see the corresponding measures in column 1 and also footnote 6 in Chapter 4.

It is possible that these findings reflect the predictive value and usefulness to forecasters of data on investment anticipations. Most of the end-of-year forecasts can and do use the figures from the McGraw-Hill Survey of Investment Intentions, which is conducted annually and released in November. However, company forecast B and also the group forecasts D and E are made in October, that is, before the release of this survey. It is particularly interesting here to compare the performance of sets B and F, which are generally similar in over-all quality. As shown in Table 17, the errors in forecasts of gross private domestic investment were much larger for set B than for set F (the $M$ values are 13.4 and 7.5, respectively, see lines 3 and 11, column 1) and most of this difference can be traced to the plant and equipment component of investment.[14] Whereas in forecasting consumption and the rest of GNP other than fixed investment the errors in set B are either smaller than, or about the same as in set F, in predicting GNP as a whole, set F is appreciably better than set B. This is clearly because of its superiority in the investment sector, which very likely reflects the fact that set F did, whereas set B did not, utilize the investment anticipations data.

In this connection, it is also interesting to note that the base-period estimates (ECP) are often considerably better for business capital outlays than for other GNP components. This, too, is probably due in large measure to the availability of anticipations surveys, including the quarterly ones made jointly by the Commerce Department's Office of Business Economics and the Securities and Exchange Commission (OBE-SEC).

The OBE-SEC *annual* surveys are conducted in January–February and published in March; hence, they provide, in effect, shorter-span predictions than those made by our forecasters at earlier dates, between October and January. The predictive record of these survey data is as good as it is partly because of their relatively short horizon. Even so, it is significant that they show much higher correlations with expenditures on producers' durables and nonresidential construction than the global investment forecasts in our collection do.[15] Such com-

[14] Compare the errors of set B in plant and equipment (Table 17, line 4) with the errors of set F in producers' durables and nonresidential construction (lines 16 and 17). The differences in favor of set F persist when the errors are recomputed for 1956–63, the period in which these forecasts overlap.

[15] The forecast and actual values are for the GNP components representing private "fixed investment," that is, the sum of the above two categories of expendi-

parisons, though inevitably crude, provide some additional evidence of the relative success of anticipations data for fixed investment.[16]

## FORECASTS AND EXTRAPOLATIONS OVER VARYING SPANS

While average forecast errors nearly always increase with the lengthening of the predictive span, the $R_1$ ratios show no definite tendency to rise along with the span (Table 18). This is so because the errors of base-level extrapolations also grow larger as the period over which the extrapolations are made is lengthened. The same applies to the $R_2$ ratios, which are not shown in the table (they are, in most cases here, smaller than $R_1$, contrary to the case for the annual GNP forecasts).[17]

On the whole, the $R_1$ ratios do not vary greatly for the different spans. In some cases, particularly for industrial production, they do increase appreciably when applied to longer forecasts (Table 18, lines 23 or 35). Elsewhere, counterexamples are found, however: a longer forecast, despite its larger average error, may be better than a shorter one when judged by comparison with a naive model (lines 8, 11, and 17). The ratios are all less than one, that is, the errors of extrapolations N1 increase with the span sufficiently to remain on the average larger than the errors of the forecasts proper.

The $R_2$* and $R_3$ ratios are all considerably larger than either $R_1$ or $R_2$. When two lagged terms are used in the N3 autoregressions, the results tend to be inferior to those of the trend projections N2* (i.e., $R_3 < R_2$* in most cases). But the differences between these ratios are on the whole small, and inclusion of additional lags should here and

ture. The anticipations data are based on a somewhat different concept which excludes private nonbusiness institutions, capital outlays charged to current expense, and some other items. In terms of levels, therefore, forecasts have smaller errors than anticipations when both are compared with the investment components of GNP; but this, of course, merely reflects differences in measurement, not in predictive performance. What is meaningful, however, is that the anticipations data (Z) show higher correlations with the recorded fixed investment outlays (I) than the global forecasts (P) do. Moreover, forecasts hardly add anything to a statistical explanation of the variance of I after allowing for the high correlation between I and Z. The partial correlation coefficients $r_{IP.Z}$ are in all cases small absolutely and a few are negative, while the values of $r_{IZ.P}$ are all positive and relatively high.

[16] Several recent writings offer substantial evidence that the expectations or intentions of business management regarding fixed investment have direct and considerable predictive value. See, e.g., the essays in *The Quality and Economic Significance of Anticipations Data* (Princeton for the National Bureau of Economic Research, 1960), particularly those by Dexter M. Keezer, *et al.* (pp. 369–386), and Arthur M. Okun (pp. 407–460).

[17] When shorter time units are used, as in the chained forecasts, the advantage that N2 has for the smoother annual series is largely lost.

## TABLE 18

### Forecasts of GNP and Industrial Production: Comparisons with Two Extrapolative Models over Spans from Three to Eighteen Months, 1947-63

| Line | Forecast Set[a] | Period Covered | Error Statistics[b] | Span of Forecast (months) | | | | | |
|---|---|---|---|---|---|---|---|---|---|
| | | | | Three (1) | Six (2) | Nine (3) | Twelve (4) | Fifteen (5) | Eighteen (6) |
| | | | | *Gross National Product* | | | | | |
| 1. | A | 1947–49, 1955–56, 1958–63 | $M$ | | 15.3 | | 24.2 | | |
| 2. | A | 1947–49, 1955–56, 1958–63 | $R_1$ | | .680 | | .752 | | |
| 3. | A | 1947–49, 1955–56, 1958–63 | $R_{2^*}$ | | 1.107 | | 1.568 | | |
| 4. | C[c] | 1958–63 | $M$ | 7.5 | 10.8 | 12.3 | 15.0 | 19.5 | |
| 5. | C[c] | 1958–63 | $R_1$ | .412 | .456 | .413 | .417 | .428 | |
| 6. | C[c] | 1958–63 | $R_{2^*}$ | .610 | .793 | .904 | 1.086 | 1.127 | |
| 7. | D | 1956–63 | $M$ | | 12.6 | | 18.1 | | |
| 8. | D | 1956–63 | $R_1$ | | .549 | | .527 | | |
| 9. | D | 1956–63 | $R_{2^*}$ | | .983 | | 1.136 | | |

*(continued)*

## TABLE 18 *(continued)*

| Line | Forecast Set[a] | Period Covered | Error Statistics[b] | Span of Forecast (months) | | | | | |
|---|---|---|---|---|---|---|---|---|---|
| | | | | Three (1) | Six (2) | Nine (3) | Twelve (4) | Fifteen (5) | Eighteen (6) |
| | | | | *Gross National Product* | | | | | |
| 10. | D | 1959–63 | M | 8.2 | 12.8 | 13.9 | 15.9 | | |
| 11. | D | 1959–63 | $R_1$ | .397 | .445 | .421 | .392 | | |
| 12. | D | 1959–63 | $R_2*$ | .763 | .874 | .962 | 1.043 | | |
| 13. | E | 1956, 1960–63 | M | | 11.9 | | 23.0 | | |
| 14. | E | 1956, 1960–63 | $R_1$ | | .475 | | .582 | | |
| 15. | E | 1956, 1960–63 | $R_2*$ | | 1.310 | | 1.807 | | |
| 16. | $G^d$ | 1955–63 | M | 8.4 | 10.0 | 13.8 | 15.4 | 17.1 | 17.0 |
| 17. | $G^d$ | 1955–63 | $R_1$ | .520 | .445 | .552 | .534 | .571 | .504 |
| 18. | $G^d$ | 1955–63 | $R_2*$ | .764 | .680 | .874 | .920 | 1.040 | 1.016 |

*(continued)*

TABLE 18 *(continued)*

| Line | Forecast Set[a] | Period Covered | Error Statistics[b] | Span of Forecast (months) | | | | | |
|---|---|---|---|---|---|---|---|---|---|
| | | | | Three (1) | Six (2) | Nine (3) | Twelve (4) | Fifteen (5) | Eighteen (6) |
| | | | | *Industrial Production* | | | | | |
| 19. | A | 1947–49, 1955–56, 1958–63 | $M$ | | 6.4 | | 7.0 | | |
| 20. | A | 1947–49, 1955–56, 1958–63 | $R_1$ | | .663 | | .651 | | |
| 21. | A | 1947–49, 1955–56, 1958–63 | $R_2*$ | | .792 | | .780 | | |
| 22. | C[c] | 1958–63 | $M$ | 4.4 | 5.6 | 6.4 | 7.0 | 9.7 | |
| 23. | C[c] | 1958–63 | $R_1$ | .529 | .571 | .592 | .605 | .681 | |
| 24. | C[c] | 1958–63 | $R_2*$ | .546 | .662 | .833 | .997 | 1.266 | |
| 25. | D | 1947–63 | $M$ | | 5.0 | | 9.0 | | |
| 26. | D | 1947–63 | $R_1$ | | .708 | | .801 | | |
| 27. | D | 1947–63 | $R_2*$ | | .670 | | .815 | | |

*(continued)*

TABLE 18 (concluded)

| Line | Forecast Set [a] | Period Covered | Error Statistics [b] | Span of Forecast (months) | | | | | |
|---|---|---|---|---|---|---|---|---|---|
| | | | | Three (1) | Six (2) | Nine (3) | Twelve (4) | Fifteen (5) | Eighteen (6) |
| | | | | *Industrial Production* | | | | | |
| 28. | D | 1959–63 | $M$ | 4.8 | 6.4 | 8.2 | 7.1 | | |
| 29. | D | 1959–63 | $R_1$ | .577 | .600 | .640 | .527 | | |
| 30. | D | 1959–63 | $R_{2*}$ | .613 | .710 | .794 | .752 | | |
| 31. | E | 1951–63 | $M$ | | 8.0 | | 7.8 | | |
| 32. | E | 1951–63 | $R_1$ | | .889 | | .749 | | |
| 33. | E | 1951–63 | $R_{2*}$ | | .790 | | .655 | | |
| 34. | G | 1956–63 | $M$ | 4.0 | 4.9 | 8.1 | 9.7 | 10.4 | 9.6 |
| 35. | G | 1956–63 | $R_1$ | .678 | .605 | .818 | .858 | .839 | .678 |
| 36. | G | 1956–63 | $R_{2*}$ | .684 | .620 | .853 | .924 | .954 | .800 |

*Notes to Table 18*

[a]All measures refer to level forecasts. The forecast sets are the same as those in Table 9, with two exceptions: (1) for GNP, a subset of D was added covering the years 1953-63, with sixteen observations per span (lines 7-9); (2) for industrial production, another subset of D was added covering the years 1947-63, with thirty-three observations per span (lines 25-27). For further details, see Table 9.

[b]The meaning of the Symbols is as follows:

$M = \sqrt{\frac{1}{n} \Sigma (P-A)^2}$ , which is the root mean square error of forecast (in billion dollars for GNP; in index points, 1947-49 = 100, for industrial production).

$R_1 = M/M_{N1}$ ; $R_2 = M/M_{N2*}$ . These are the root mean square error ratios of forecast to extrapolation.

[c]The entries on this line are not strictly comparable because some of the forecast chains are "incomplete," so that the number of observations for different spans varies. See Table 9, note b.

[d]Based on forecasts in constant prices, as reported, and on corresponding extrapolations.

there tip the scales in favor of N3 (the evidence on this point is still incomplete).

In most cases the $R_2*$ ratios show increases when the predictive span is extended (Table 18). This means that the N2* extrapolations do not deteriorate as much as the forecasts proper, so that their relative performance improves as spans lengthen. It should be noted that the same applies to the autoregressive predictions: the $R_3$ ratios also tend to rise for the longer forecasts. Model N3 does indeed suggest the likelihood of this result.[18]

[18] Suppose that $A_t = a + b A_{t-1} + u_t$. Then $A_{t+1} = a + b A_t + u_{t+1} = a(1 + b) + b^2 A_{t-1} + (bu_t + u_{t+1})$. Over the span of one period, the variance of the residuals is var $(u_t)$; over two periods, it is var $(bu_t + u_{t+1})$ which, assuming that the $u$'s are independent and have equal variances, equals $(1 + b^2)$ var $(u)$. Thus the variance increases with the span, depending on the size of $b$. This is illustrated here in the simplest case of a first-order autoregression, but the same argument applies to more complex situations.

Extrapolations for increasing spans are derived by stepwise "chaining" of predicted and observed values as follows. Let the forecast for one quarter ahead be $\hat{A}_t = a + b_1 A_{t-1} + b_2 A_{t-2} \cdots$ ; for two quarters, $\hat{A}_{t+1} = a + b_1 \hat{A}_t + b_2 A_{t-1} \cdots$ ; etc. The coefficients $a$, $b_1$, $b_2 \cdots$ are estimated in the first step (which may

For two sets of GNP forecasts, the $R_2{}^*$ ratios are all larger than one (lines 3 and 15), indicating that here both the six- and the twelve-month predictions are on the whole worse than the average change extrapolations over the periods covered.[19] For other sets, the $R_2{}^*$ ratios are less than one for the short spans, but they approach or exceed one for the longer spans (mostly nine to fifteen months, in one case fifteen to eighteen months; see Table 18, lines 6, 12, and 18).

For industrial production, the ratios grow smaller as the spans lengthen. Our table includes only three instances of $R_2{}^* > 0.9$ and only one of $R_2{}^* > 1.0$, all in the range of twelve- to fifteen-month forecasts (lines 24 and 36).

Presumably, the observed association between longer forecasts and larger errors can be partly explained by the fact that extrapolations of various types also tend to worsen as the predictive span lengthens. The past behavior of the series to be predicted will usually be considered in some way by the forecaster, and many explicitly use various extrapolative techniques. Forecast and extrapolation often have much in common, and the latter may be viewed as one of the ingredients of the former.[20] However, forecasters apparently fail to use the historical content of the series as efficiently as they might even by fairly simple and inexpensive means, perhaps because they pay too much attention to the very few values in the most recent past. Better use of trend projections would have improved many forecasts, particularly those of GNP over longer spans. This can be inferred from the comparisons of forecasts with the N2* model. As shown earlier, the growth of the economy has often been underestimated in the forecasts, an error that simple trend extrapolations would have helped to reduce.

---

relate to the fourth quarter of the base year, ECP) and retained in the following steps for the given multiperiod forecast (say, for the estimation of the four quarters of the next year).

Some experiments were also made with another approach, consisting of separate fittings for different spans: regressions of $A_t, A_{t+1}, \cdots A_{t+4}$ on $A_{t-1}, A_{t-2} \cdots$ (this gives five equations for each year covered by the predictions). It is interesting that the two approaches gave very similar results for GNP. In general, however, the chained forecasts are more accurate than the fits by span.

[19] As will be shown later, the results of such comparisons depend on the periods covered. It should be noted that one of these sets (A) includes the early postwar years, 1947–49, for which forecasts were particularly poor.

[20] Statistical methods, e.g., partial correlation analysis, can help evaluate this relation; work along these lines is in process (see footnote 2 above).

Other ingredients of forecasts may, to be sure, also contribute to the decreasing accuracy of longer-range predictions. These ingredients —variables that typically move in advance of the predicted series, anticipations data, and the forecasters' own judgment—also are probably decreasingly reliable over longer spans.

NEAR-TERM FORESIGHT AND ACCURACY OF
ANNUAL PREDICTIONS

We find, then, that forecasts of the near future are definitely superior to all types of extrapolation, while forecasts with longer spans, of nine or twelve months and more, are not (they are in fact worse than some extrapolations). Let us also recall that the year-to-year forecasts proved generally better than extrapolations. Are these findings consistent? Does the record of the annual forecasts imply greater accuracy than that of the forecasts with varying spans?

The answers are yes to the first question and no to the second. The annual forecasts are generally made late in the preceding calendar year. They can be viewed as averages of the quarterly or semiannual forecasts and some are actually so computed; their mean spans, then, are roughly six months (or again somewhat more than that for the "effective span"). Errors of the (explicit or implicit) forecasts for parts of the year could in some degree be mutually offsetting, which would tend to make the annual forecasts better than most of the shorter ones. This seems, indeed, to be true in some cases. On the whole, however, annual forecasts definitely tend to be better only relative to the forecasts for the late parts of the year, not to those for the early parts.

Furthermore, a good predictive record for the first two quarters would be sufficient to produce a moderately good record for the year as a whole. Even the knowledge of the first quarter alone would make a substantial contribution to the quality of annual forecasts of GNP. This is indicated by some experiments we have performed following a suggestion by Geoffrey Moore. These show, in effect, that if one knew what the early parts of the next year would bring and extrapolated this information in simple ways, the resulting annual forecasts would compare very well indeed with the actual forecasts we have examined.

We proceed by constructing hypothetical *"ex-post forecasts"* incorporating information about parts of the predicted future, which is regarded as free of errors. The first assumption is that the forecaster has full knowledge of the level of the series in the fourth quarter of the base year (ECP) and in the first quarter of the coming year. Three types of extrapolations are then applied successively. (1) The level of the series next year is taken simply as equal to the first quarter's level expressed at the annual rate. This extrapolation, a variant of N1, will be called $XQ_1$. (2) It is assumed that the level in the second quarter will differ from that in the first by the amount of the last "known" change (which here is that from the fourth quarter of the current year to the first quarter of the next year); also, that the third quarter will differ from the second, and the fourth quarter from the third, by the same amounts. This leads to a variant of the N2 model, to be denoted as $XQ_{\Delta 1}$. (3) Incorporating the assumed knowledge of the current and coming quarter, the mean historical change in the series is computed and projected to obtain the predictions of the three remaining quarters of the next year. This is a variant of the N2* model and it is labeled $XQ_{\Delta 1}*$.

The second assumption about the available degree of foresight is that, in addition to ECP and the first quarter, the level of the series in the second quarter of the coming year is also known. Again, the three types of extrapolations are applied, in analogy to N1, N2, and N2*, respectively, which yields the following models. (4) The series is assumed to remain at its second quarter's level in both the third and the fourth quarter ($XQ_2$). (5) The series is assumed to change in the third quarter by the ("known") amount of its change in the second quarter, and the change in the fourth quarter is also set as equal to the same amount ($XQ_{\Delta 2}$). (6) The average change in the series is computed from the past record, including in addition the changes in the first half of the coming year, the knowledge of which is imputed to the forecaster. The projection of this amount of change over the second half of the year is used to construct annual predictions $XQ_{\Delta 2}*$.[21]

21 Let the values of a series in quarter IV of the current year and in quarters I and II of the predicted year, expressed at annual rates, be $A_0$, $A_1$, and $A_2$. Let the average historical change incorporating quarters IV and I be $\overline{\Delta A}(1)$ and the corresponding measure incorporating quarters IV, I, and II be $\overline{\Delta A}(2)$. Then the six experiments can be described as follows:

(1) $$XQ_1 \;=\; A_1$$

(2) $$XQ_{\Delta 1} \;=\; \frac{4\,A_1 + 6\,(A_1 - A_0)}{4} = \frac{5\,A_1 - 3\,A_0}{2}$$

The results of applying these models of *ex-post* projections to both GNP and industrial production are summarized in Table 19. As shown there, three forecasts covering the years 1953–63 managed to do better than the simple last-level and last-change extrapolations of the coming year's first quarter, $XQ_1$ and $XQ_{\Delta 1}$ (compare lines 1 and 2 with lines 8–10). For industrial production, the forecasts are even somewhat better than the trend extrapolation $XQ_{\Delta 1}^*$, but for GNP the reverse is true (lines 3 and 8–10).

Those extrapolations that use the second quarter as well are generally superior to the forecasts of GNP. For industrial production, $XQ_2$ and $XQ_{\Delta 2}^*$ also score better than the forecasts, but the differences are smaller here and at least one forecast comes out ahead of $XQ_{\Delta 2}$ (compare lines 4–6 and 8–10).

The trend extrapolations tend to be better than the other models, as would be expected (one exception is that $XQ_2$ gives the best results for industrial production). The only case of decidedly poor performance is $XQ_{\Delta 1}$ for GNP (see lines 1–6).

As a next step, it seemed desirable to relax the strong assumption of perfect knowledge which underlies these models. We replace the actual values for the early part of the predicted year by reported quarterly forecasts and again use extrapolations for the rest of the year. Table 19 shows that such a combination ($GXQ_{\Delta 2}^*$), which uses forecasts for the first two quarters and trend projections for quarters III and IV, yields on the average somewhat smaller errors than the forecasts proper for GNP (compare lines 7 and 8–10). In the case of industrial production, the results are mixed: one forecast is a little worse and one better than $GXQ_{\Delta 2}^*$.

Chart 6 presents the year-by-year record of predicted changes and their

---

(3)      $$XQ_{\Delta 1}^* = \frac{4\,A_1 + 6\,\overline{\Delta A}(1)}{4} = A_1 + \frac{3}{2}\,\overline{\Delta A}(1)$$

(4)      $$XQ_2 = \frac{A_1 + 3\,A_2}{4}$$

(5)      $$XQ_{\Delta 2} = \frac{A_1 + 3\,A_2 + 3\,(A_2 - A_1)}{4} = \frac{3\,A_2 - A_1}{2}$$

(6)      $$XQ_{\Delta 2}^* = \frac{A_1 + 3\,A_2 + 3\,\overline{\Delta A}(2)}{4}$$

## TABLE 19

### Comparisons of *Annual* Ex-Post Extrapolations and Ex-Ante Forecasts of *GNP and Industrial Production, 1953-63*

| Line | Type of Extrapolation or Forecast[a] | Gross National Product (billion dollars) | | | Industrial Production (1947–49 = 100) | | |
|---|---|---|---|---|---|---|---|
| | | Mean Absolute Error, $\lvert E \rvert$ (1) | Mean Arithmetic Error, $\bar{E}$ (2) | Root Mean Square Error, $M$ (3) | Mean Absolute Error, $\lvert E \rvert$ (4) | Mean Arithmetic Error, $\bar{E}$ (5) | Root Mean Square Error, $M$ (6) |
| | Full knowledge of I $Q_{t+1}$ | | | | | | |
| 1. | $XQ_1$ | 8.6 | -8.6 | 10.1 | 4.6 | 1.7 | 5.3 |
| 2. | $XQ_{\Delta 1}$ | 21.3 | 8.3 | 22.8 | 11.1 | -0.3 | 4.9 |
| 3. | $XQ_{\Delta 1}{}^{*}$ | 4.7 | 0.1 | 5.6 | 4.5 | 1.5 | 5.0 |
| | Full knowledge of I & II $Q_{t+1}$ | | | | | | |
| 4. | $XQ_2$ | 4.1 | -3.2 | 5.0 | 2.3 | -0.1 | 2.8 |
| 5. | $XQ_{\Delta 2}$ | 3.3 | 1.4 | 4.4 | 3.5 | 0.8 | 4.2 |
| 6. | $XQ_{\Delta 2}{}^{*}$ | 3.5 | 0.7 | 4.0 | 2.5 | 0.9 | 3.2 |
| | Combined forecast-projection | | | | | | |
| 7. | $GXQ_{\Delta 2}{}^{*}$ | 6.0 | 3.2 | 7.0 | 3.5 | 1.9 | 4.1 |

*(continued)*

TABLE 19 (concluded)

| Line | Type of Extrapolation or Forecast[a] | Gross National Product (billion dollars) | | | Industrial Production (1947–49 = 100) | | |
|---|---|---|---|---|---|---|---|
| | | Mean Absolute Error, $\lvert\overline{E}\rvert$ (1) | Mean Arithmetic Error, $\overline{E}$ (2) | Root Mean Square Error, M (3) | Mean Absolute Error, $\lvert\overline{E}\rvert$ (4) | Mean Arithmetic Error, $\overline{E}$ (5) | Root Mean Square Error, M (6) |
| | End-of-year forecasts[b] | | | | | | |
| 8. | B | 8.4 | -1.3 | 9.7 | n.a. | n.a. | n.a. |
| 9. | F | 6.3 | -2.3 | 7.5 | 2.8 | -0.7 | 3.6 |
| 10. | G[c] | 7.1 | 3.0 | 7.9 | 3.6 | 1.9 | 4.3 |

[a]The models used are as follows (see text and note 21 for full explanation):

Lines 1–3: Assumes knowledge of the values of GNP or industrial production in the first quarter of the predicted year.

Lines 4–6: Assumes knowledge of the values of GNP or industrial production in the first and second quarters of the predicted year.

Line 7: Forecasts G for the first and second quarters combined with average-change extrapolations N2* for the third and fourth quarters.

[b]Measures apply to forecasts of changes, which are appropriate for these comparisons. The extrapolations assume perfect knowledge of the base-period values, hence contain no ECP errors.

[c]Made typically in terms of base-period prices; here converted to current dollars (see Table 1, note d).

## CHART 6

*Four Types of Ex-Post Extrapolations of GNP and Industrial Production, Actual and Predicted Changes and Errors, 1953–63*

—— Actual change
---- Predicted change
—— Error of predicted change

Index of Industrial Production

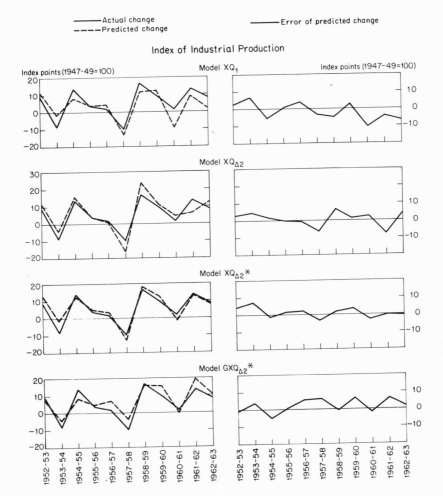

## CHART 6 (*concluded*)

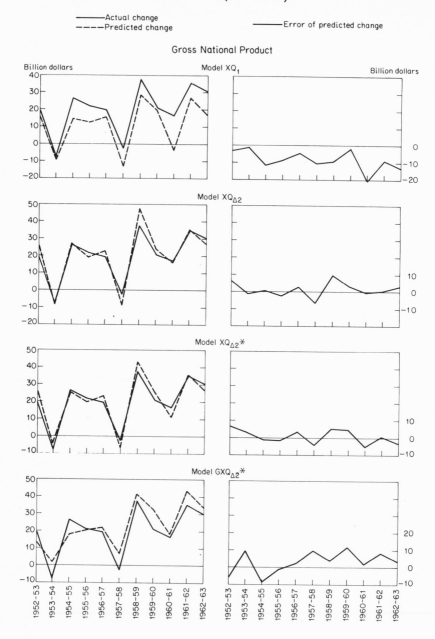

Gross National Product

errors for four of our seven experimental models.[22] This chart should be compared with Charts 1 and 2 (for the forecasts proper) and Chart 5 (for the *ex-ante* extrapolations).[23] In this way, one can observe that some similarities exist between forecasts and the first-quarter extrapolations, and that great improvements are effected by the incorporation of near-term foresight in the extrapolative models. The most dramatic improvements, in terms of bias elimination as well as reduction of the size of errors, come with the inclusion of the second quarter (which receives a dominant weight in the corresponding models, see the formulas (4)–(6) in footnote 21). The error-increasing and partly biasing effects of using forecasts instead of actual values for quarters I and II can be seen by comparing graphs for $XQ_{\Delta 2}*$ and $GXQ_{\Delta 2}*$ in Chart 6. The mild improvements resulting from the use of simple trend projections N2* instead of forecasts for quarters III and IV can only be detected with difficulty by comparing the graphs for $GXQ_{\Delta 2}*$ in Chart 6 with those for the forecast set G in Charts 1 and 2.

### SECTORAL FORECASTS AND EXTRAPOLATIONS FOR DIFFERENT SPANS

Table 20 compares forecasts of GNP components in set C with simple level and trend extrapolations. The average absolute errors of these forecasts were presented earlier (see Table 15).

The ranks of the different variables according to the over-all errors of percentage changes $(M_P)$ are relatively independent of the span. Among the shortest as well as the longer forecasts, total consumption has the smallest errors, government expenditures and consumer durables follow, and the investment variables show the largest errors.[24]

Comparisons with extrapolations yield less consistent results. According to the $R_1$ ratios, which are based on simple level projections, total

[22] For the corresponding summary measures, see Table 19, lines 1 and 5–7. The models not shown in the chart (they are listed on lines 2–4) include extreme cases such as $XQ_{\Delta 1}$, which works relatively well for the production index but poorly for GNP, and $XQ_2$, for which the reverse is true. The selection was found sufficiently illustrative for our present purpose.

[23] To facilitate such comparisons, all graphs for GNP were drawn on the same scale, and so were all graphs for the production index.

[24] The values of $M_p$ are larger for residential construction than for plant and equipment, but they are larger still for total GPDI, which suggests a major weakness of the inventory change forecasts. (The latter and the net foreign investment forecasts cannot be included in these comparisons, which refer to relative change errors.)

TABLE 20

*Forecasts of Eight Selected Components of GNP: Comparisons with Extrapolations over Spans from Three to Eighteen Months, 1958-63*

| Line | Error Statistics[a] | Span of Forecast (months) | | | | |
|---|---|---|---|---|---|---|
| | | Three (1) | Six (2) | Nine (3) | Twelve (4) | Fifteen (5) |
| | | *Personal Consumption Expenditures*[b] | | | | |
| 1. | $M_P$ (percentage points) | 0.81 | 1.12 | 1.40 | 1.70 | 2.15 |
| 2. | Ratio $R_1$ | 0.579 | 0.444 | 0.371 | 0.348 | 0.321 |
| 3. | Ratio $R_2$* | 1.052 | 1.047 | .881 | 1.156 | .964 |
| | | *Consumer Durables*[c] | | | | |
| 4. | $M_P$ (percentage points) | 4.55 | 5.01 | 5.56 | 5.77 | 9.20 |
| 5. | Ratio $R_1$ | 0.887 | 0.977 | 0.788 | .996 | 0.830 |
| 6. | Ratio $R_2$* | 0.950 | 1.029 | 0.952 | 1.607 | 1.309 |
| | | *Gross Private Domestic Investment*[b] | | | | |
| 7. | $M_P$ (percentage points) | 6.22 | 11.00 | 12.14 | 14.48 | 18.51 |
| 8. | Ratio $R_1$ | 0.772 | 0.853 | 0.796 | 1.059 | 0.836 |
| 9. | Ratio $R_2$* | 0.784 | 0.890 | 0.875 | 1.355 | 1.014 |
| | | *Plant and Equipment Outlays*[b] | | | | |
| 10. | $M_P$ (percentage points) | 3.10 | 4.77. | 6.62 | 8.41 | 10.52 |
| 11. | Ratio $R_1$ | 0.856 | 0.810 | 0.916 | 1.031 | 1.224 |
| 12. | Ratio $R$ * | 0.852 | 0.840 | 1.027 | .825 | 2.234 |
| | | *Residential Construction*[b] | | | | |
| 13. | $M_P$ (percentage points) | 5.13 | 8.91 | 8.62 | 7.97 | 8.46 |
| 14. | Ratio $R_1$ | 0.902 | 0.953 | 0.721 | 0.595 | 0.494 |
| 15. | Ratio $R_2$* | 0.914 | 1.009 | 0.845 | 0.755 | 0.636 |
| | | *Government Expenditures*[b] | | | | |
| 16. | $M_P$ (percentage points) | 1.43 | 1.72 | 2.05 | 3.00 | 2.55 |
| 17. | Ratio $R_1$ | 0.641 | 0.446 | 0.367 | 0.398 | 0.281 |
| 18. | Ratio $R_2$* | 0.734 | 0.892 | 0.894 | 0.930 | 1.002 |

*(continued)*

TABLE 20 *(concluded)*

| Line | Error Statistics[a] | Span of Forecast (months) | | | | |
|------|---------------------|-----------------|------------|-------------|---------------|-----------------|
| | | Three (1) | Six (2) | Nine (3) | Twelve (4) | Fifteen (5) |
| | | *Net Change in Inventories*[d] | | | | |
| 19. | $M_P$ (billion dollars) | 2.54 | 5.31 | 5.67 | 6.78 | 6.58 |
| 20. | Ratio $R_1$ | 0.692 | 0.881 | 0.901 | 1.292 | 0.903 |
| 21. | Ratio $R_2$* | 0.690 | 0.873 | 0.889 | 1.317 | 0.899 |
| | | *Net Foreign Balance*[b] | | | | |
| 22. | $M_P$ (billion dollars) | 1.09 | 1.35 | 1.38 | 1.51 | 1.73 |
| 23. | Ratio $R_1$ | 1.072 | 0.928 | 0.766 | 0.686 | 0.736 |
| 24. | Ratio $R_2$* | 1.048 | 0.894 | 0.730 | 0.659 | 0.721 |

[a]$M_P$ denotes the root mean square error of forecast; $R_1$ and $R_2$ denote the root mean square error ratios of forecast to extrapolation (see the formulae in Table 18, note 6).

[b]Forecasts cover the period 1958–63. The numbers of observations are 21, 20, 19, 13, and 7 for spans of 3, 6, 9, 12, and 15 months, respectively. The numbers vary because some of the forecast chains do not include all spans (see Table 9, note b).

[c]Forecasts cover the period 1961–63. The numbers of observations for spans of 3 to 15 months are 13, 11, 10, 7, and 4.

[d]Forecasts cover the period 1958–63. The numbers of observations for spans of 3 to 15 months are 19, 17, 16, 10, and 5.

consumption again has the best record (lowest ratios), followed by governmental expenditures; but consumption of durable goods performs no better here than the investment variables. In agreement with the findings for the annual figures, comparisons with simple trend extrapolations are very unfavorable to the consumption forecasts. Most of the $R_2$* ratios exceed one for both total consumer expenditures and spending on consumer durables, and this includes the short as well as the longer forecasts (Table 20, lines 3 and 6). In fact, these ratios tend to be larger for consumption than for any other major GNP component.

The $R_2^*$ ratios are generally high; 35 per cent of them exceed unity (there is at least one case of $R_2^* > 1.0$ for each of the variables); 25 per cent fall into the range 0.80–0.99; and the remaining 20 per cent are all above 0.6.

The $R_1$ ratios are as a rule smaller, but they are often sizable. While no more than one-eighth of them exceed 1.0, only about one-fourth are less than 0.6.

The margins by which $R_2^*$ exceed $R_1$ are particularly large for series with strong trends such as consumption, as would be expected. By the same token, the two ratios are closely similar for series in which trends are unimportant, such as net change in inventories and net foreign balance. Also, the margins in favor of $R_2^*$ often increase with the span of forecast—which presumably reflects the fact that trends are more important over longer periods of time.

Table 20 shows a tendency for the $R_2^*$ ratios to increase with the predictive span in most cases, but not always. Where the ratios rise, they do so irregularly (the only exception is the forecast span of government spending on line 18). For two variables, residential construction and net foreign balance, the ratios are actually higher for the short forecasts than for the longer ones (lines 15 and 24).

There is no reason to expect uniformity in the relation between forecasts and extrapolations for different spans when comparing results for variables with very different characteristics. Such comparisons can be instructive, but additional data are needed at this point and they are hard to get. The available evidence leaves much to be desired, since forecasts C cover a short period of time and their number varies for different spans (see notes to Table 20).

### TURNING-POINT ERRORS AND EXTRAPOLATIONS

The use of extrapolative criteria in the appraisal of forecasts has certain implications for turning-point errors. To reconsider the latter, the concepts and notation introduced in the last section of Chapter 4 must be recalled.

A forecast that never predicted any turning points would, of course, have a zero score on "hits" ($TT = 0$), but also a zero score on false signals ($NT = 0$).[25] On the other hand, by missing all the actual turns, such a forecast would have the worst possible score on errors of the second kind: its $\bar{E}_{T2}$ ratio ($= \dfrac{TN}{TN + TT}$) would equal one. Benchmark forecasts based on extrapolations of the most recent levels or changes or of trends (N1, N2, N2*) do not predict turning points and have, therefore, exactly these characteristics.

The other extreme is represented by a model that predicts a turning point on each occasion. Such a forecast would miss no turns ($TN = 0$) but would have the largest possible number of false signals. Here $NT$ would equal the number of all periods in which there were no observed turns, and the $\bar{E}_{T1}$ ratio would be correspondingly at the maximum.

The built-in disadvantage of forecasts vis-à-vis extrapolations with respect to false warnings may or may not be outweighed by the potential advantage of making correct turning-point predictions. It is difficult to decide what weights to attach to the two kinds of error without information on costs of missed turns vs. false signals to the forecast user.

One simple criterion, implying equal weights, is that the total number of errors of either kind ($n_e = NT + TN$) be less than the total number of turns recorded ($n_a = TT + TN$). The requirement that $n_e < n_a$ reduces to $NT < TT$. In simple extrapolations, of course, $n_e = n_a$, because $NT = 0$ and $TN = n_a$.[26]

However, it could be argued that forecasts for which $n_e = n_a$ may be better than extrapolations, even if they show no fewer errors of both kinds, if they correctly predict at least some turning points (since then $TT > 0$, whereas for the extrapolations $TT$ is always zero).

For ten of the forecast sets listed in Table 8, the condition $n_e < n_a$ is satisfied. In the five remaining cases, $n_e = n_a$.

All measures based on the proportion of errors in the turning-point forecasts, that is, on some combinations of $\bar{E}_{T1}$ and $\bar{E}_{T2}$, are of course functions of $TN$, $NT$, and $TT$ only. They disregard $NN$, the fre-

---

[25] Thus all terms in the ratio of false signals, $\bar{E}_{T1} = \dfrac{NT}{NT + TT}$, would in this case equal zero, making the expression indeterminate.

[26] In the model which predicts a turn on each occasion, $n_e = NT$ and $n_a = TT$ (since $TN = NN = 0$). The criterion $n_e < n_a$, therefore, simply describes for this model the requirement that successes be more numerous than failures. The model will meet this requirement if and only if $n_a > 1/2n$, where $n$ is the total number of forecasts ($= n_a + n_e$).

quency of those periods in which neither the predicted nor the actual values showed a change in direction. The simplest measure that would take $NN$ into account is $\bar{E}_T = \dfrac{NT + TN}{n} = \dfrac{n_e}{n_e + n_s}$, where $n_s$ is the number of all directionally correct predictions ($= NN + TT$) and $n$ the number of all predictions covered. The $\bar{E}_T$ ratios for the forecasts in Table 8 range from 0 to 0.24 and average about 0.12 (that is, the over-all proportion of turning-point error is 12 per cent).

The proportion of turning points observed in the past, $n_a/n$, is known to the forecaster but is of little help to him, even if it is accepted as the best forecast of the proportion that will prevail in the future. This expected value is a fraction, but the forecaster must decide on each occasion whether or not a directional change is about to occur: he can either predict one or not but he cannot predict a fraction. Suppose that he adopts the following decision rule: never predict a turn for a series which shows $n_a/n < 1/2$ and always predict a turn for a series which shows $n_a/n > 1/2$. This would amount to the use of the first of our two extreme benchmark models in the former case and of the second one in the latter case. But the proportions of predicted turns would then be 0 and 1, respectively, and they would probably be poor approximations to the true fraction $n_a/n$ in either case.

Clearly, it is not satisfactory to compare the forecasts with these limiting alternatives only. An extrapolative benchmark model is needed, which could produce turning points depending on the configurations of previous increases and decreases in the series concerned. Autoregressive models which incorporate several lagged terms can in principle meet this need.

The results of the annual N3 extrapolations for GNP and industrial production are, however, distinctly unfavorable with respect to predictions of the direction of change, as shown for the five-lag models in Chart 3. For GNP, no declines were indicated by the model in either 1954 or 1958, but a slight decline was predicted for 1960, a year in which GNP flattened off in another mild recession but did not fall relative to the preceding year. This record containing two missed turns and one false signal (in comparison with the early estimates) is much worse than that of the forecasts proper, which show no more than one missed turn in the same period. And for industrial production the performance of the model shown in Chart 3 was still weaker. Here the model predicted negative changes in six of the eleven years but only once correctly (for 1954). Again, failures of this magnitude are in general not observable among the forecasts proper.

Evidence on these and other comparisons between forecasts and extrapolations is presented in Table 21. Here the over-all percentages of directional errors ($\bar{E}_T$) are listed for several sets of reported forecasts and constructed benchmark predictions relating to some of the major expenditure series as well as to total GNP and industrial production. It turns out that the performance of N3 with several lagged terms is in most cases inferior to that of other extrapolative models, such as N2* and N3 with but one or two lags (the reverse is true only for plant and equipment outlays; compare columns 1–4, lines 11–15). The addition of lagged terms in the N3 model appears to often have the effect of causing "extra" turns, which both N2* and N3, with fewer lags, avoid.

Comparing the results obtained for different variables, we find that they suggest the following. (1) The frequency of turning-point errors tends to be considerably larger in extrapolations than in forecasts for GNP and, particularly, for industrial production. (2) Directional errors are much more numerous in predictions of gross private domestic investment, and this applies to both forecasts proper and extrapolations. There is some evidence here that forecasters, by and large, did a little better than the adopted benchmark models, but it is certainly not conclusive. For plant and equipment outlays, for example, some of the evidence points in the opposite direction (see lines 4, 5, 13, and 14). (3) Forecasts of consumption show very few turning-point errors, and most sets show no such errors at all. The trend and autoregressive extrapolations N2* and N3 produced no errors of direction for this series which, it will be recalled, was fairly smooth and growing from year to year in the period concerned (see lines 2 and 12).

Some other measures pertaining to forecasts only provide further indications that directional errors are particularly frequent for highly volatile series that show large changes which can vary in sign. This is so for the net change in business inventories and, very markedly, for

## TABLE 21

### Directional Errors in Selected Annual Forecasts and Extrapolations of GNP and Components and Industrial Production, 1953-63

(per cent)

| Line | Predicted Variable | Forecast Sets and Periods Covered[a] | | | |
|---|---|---|---|---|---|
| | | B 1953-63(11) (1) | F 1953-63(11) (2) | A 1958-63(6)[b] (3) | C 1958-63(6) (4) |
| 1. | Gross national product | 9.1 | 0 | 10.0[c] | 16.7 |
| 2. | Consumption expenditures | 0 | 9.1 | 0 | 0 |
| 3. | Gross private domestic investment | 27.3 | 9.1 | 33.3 | 0 |
| 4. | Plant and equipment outlays | 30.0[d] | n.a. | n.a. | 0 |
| 5. | Producer's durable equipment | n.a. | 11.1[e] | 16.7 | n.a. |
| 6. | New construction | n.a. | 50.0[f] | 0 | n.a. |
| 7. | Inventory change | 14.3[g] | 30.0[d] | 20.0[h] | 16.7 |
| 8. | Net foreign balance | 20.0[h] | 30.0[d] | 50.0 | 33.3 |
| 9. | Government expenditures | 9.1 | 0 | 0 | 0 |
| 10. | Industrial production index | n.a. | 9.1 | 10.0 | 16.7 |

(continued)

TABLE 21 *(concluded)*

| Line | Predicted Variable | N2*<br>1953–63(11) | Extrapolative Models [i] | | | |
|------|--------------------|--------------------|-----------------------------------|-----------------------------------|-------------------------------|--------------------------------|
| | | | N3 (1–2 terms)<br>1953–63(11) | N3 (2–5 terms)<br>1953–63(11) | N3 (range)[j]<br>1958–63(6) |
| 11. | Gross national product | 18.2 | 18.2 | 27.3 | 16.7 – 33.3 |
| 12. | Consumption expenditures | 0 | 0 | 0 | 0 |
| 13. | Gross private domestic investment | 27.3 | 27.3 | 36.4 | 33.3 – 50.0 |
| 14. | Plant and equipment outlays[d] | 20.0 | 22.2 | 10.0 | 0 |
| 15. | Industrial production index | 18.2 | 36.4 | 54.5 | 33.3 – 66.7 |

[a]Numbers of observations are given in parentheses following the specification of periods covered. Cases in which the numbers differ are identified in notes c–i.

[b]These refer to the last quarter of the next year, not to the total for the year (except for 1958).

[c]Refers to the period 1954–63 (10 years). The figure for 1958–63 is 16.3 per cent.

[d]Refers to the period 1953–62 (10 years).

[e]Based on nine observations.

[f]Based on eight observations.

[g]Based on seven observations.

[h]Based on five observations.

[i]Include the average-change projections N2* and autoregressive extrapolations N3 based on 1–5 lagged terms (see text for explanation of these models). The entries in column 2 refer to N3 with 1 or 2 terms (i.e., to extrapolations of the relationship between $A_t$ and $A_{t-i}$, where $i = 1, 2$) and the entries in column 3 refer to N3 with 2–5 terms ($i = 2 \ldots 5$). The results in columns 1–3 cover the period 1953–63 and are therefore comparable to those shown for the forecast sets B and F in lines 1–4 and 10, columns 1 and 2.

[j]These figures refer to the period 1958–63 and are comparable with those shown for forecast sets A and C in lines 1–4 and 10, columns 3 and 4. Where two entries are given, the first one pertains to N3 models with fewer terms ($i = 1, 2, 3$) and the second one to models with more terms ($i = 2 \ldots 5$). Elsewhere (lines 12 and 14), the same result was obtained for each of the five N3 models used.

net foreign investment (lines 7 and 8). On the other hand, forecasts of government expenditures, like those of consumption, show very few or no directional errors (line 9).[27]

[27] The statements in this and the preceding paragraph are based on considerably more evidence than the selection presented in Table 21. In each case both forecasts and extrapolations were compared with the same set of "actual" data, which, as elsewhere, consist of the early vintage estimates available on an annual basis in the first quarter following the year to which the forecasts refer.

# 7

# COMPARATIVE ADVANTAGES
# OF TYPES OF FORECASTS

### ADVANTAGES OF EXPERTISE IN SECTORAL FORECASTS

For one of the forecast sets (A) it is possible to compare three methods of arriving at a forecast of GNP. Each of the participants submits a forecast of total GNP. The mean of these forecasts, which we now designate A(M), is the set used for group A so far in our tables. In addition, each of the members of the group forecasts a particular sector or aspect of the economy. By consolidating these forecasts of each expenditure sector of GNP (personal consumption, government spending, etc.), a single forecast of total GNP is obtained, to be denoted A(S). The third procedure is to project the trend in real potential GNP with the aid of labor force and productivity estimates and to adjust the result by means of the average group A forecasts of unemployment and prices. The forecast thus derived will be called A(L). The forecasts A(S) and A(L) are available for semiannual or annual periods in 1955–58 and for the fourth quarters of the coming year since 1959. In Table 22, they are compared with each other and with some other fourth-quarter forecasts.

Among the three methods, the sum-of-sectors forecast A(S) has the smallest average error, followed by the labor-input productivity forecast A(L), while A(M) ranks third in terms of both level and change errors. The superiority of A(S) and A(L) over A(M) is sufficient to make their average errors smaller than those for the other forecasts for which we have a comparable record.[1] As between the A(S) and A(L) models, while the former produced smaller absolute errors, the latter

---

[1] Incidentally, the fourth-quarter forecasts on which the comparison is based have in general substantially larger errors than the annual forecasts made at the same time (which would be expected, of course, since their spans are longer).

## TABLE 22

*Selected Summary Measures of Error in GNP Forecasts of*
*Fourth Quarter of Following Year, 1955-63 and 1959-63*

(billion dollars)

| Line | Forecast Set[a] | Forecasts of Levels | | | Forecasts of Changes, |
|------|------|------|------|------|------|
| | | Mean Absolute Error, $\overline{|E|}$ | Mean Error, $\overline{E}$ | Root Mean Square Error $(M_P)$ | Root Mean Square Error $(M_P)$ |
| | | (1) | (2) | (3) | (4) |
| | | *Period Covered: 1959-63[b]* | | | |
| 1. | A(M) | 14.4 | −7.1 | 16.6 | 15.8 |
| 2. | A(S) | 10.4 | −8.6 | 12.4 | 10.1 |
| 3. | A(L) | 11.5 | −2.9 | 14.1 | 14.7 |
| 4. | C | 14.0 | −1.1 | 15.2 | 16.3 |
| 5. | D | 16.6 | −10.1 | 19.2 | 18.5 |
| 6. | E | 18.2 | −13.4 | 21.0 | 20.8 |
| 7. | G | 15.6 | +12.9 | 17.2 | 20.2 |
| | | *Period Covered: 1955-63[c]* | | | |
| 8. | A(M) | 14.2 | −9.8 | 17.3 | 15.0 |
| 9. | A(S) | 10.6 | −8.0 | 13.2 | 10.8 |
| 10. | A(L) | 10.7 | −5.1 | 13.7 | 12.8 |

[a] A(M): group mean forecast for set A; A(S): sum-of-sectors forecast for A; A(L): labor-input productivity forecast for A. See text on these models. The rest of the code is familiar from the tables and text above.

[b] All the forecasts refer to the fourth quarters of the year. The number of forecasts was five.

[c] The forecasts for 1955-56 refer to the second half of the year; those for 1957-58, to the year as a whole; and those for 1959-63, to the fourth quarter of the year. The number of forecasts was nine.

apparently avoided much of the underestimation bias of the other forecasts by allowing more strongly and more accurately for the upward trend in GNP.

Thus the sum-of-sector forecasts by the group's experts in the particular fields prove, on the average, superior to the mean of the global forecasts of GNP by all the individuals in the group. It is important to distinguish this situation from the one considered earlier, where total GNP forecasts were compared with sectoral forecasts by the same individuals or groups. There it was recognized that partial cancellation of errors in the aggregation by sectors helped explain the smaller over-all errors in the GNP forecast than in most of the component forecasts. But here we compare two alternative forecasts with the same degree of aggregation, both of which are presumably helped by the offsetting sectoral errors. If A(S) is better than A(M), this suggests that the sectoral forecasts by individual experts contained in A(S) are more accurate than the mean sectoral forecasts of all the group members contained in A(M). Since these same individuals also participate in the A(M) forecasts, one can also say that their predictions in the particular areas assigned to them apparently have been better than their predictions in the other areas.

This result, therefore, suggests that reliance on expertise in particular sectors may yield better forecasts. However, our evidence is scanty and it would be desirable to develop further data bearing on this point.

### AGGREGATE AND INDIVIDUAL FORECASTS

For one large group of business economists, whose forecasts are designated as set D, an intensive analysis was made of the individual member forecasts as well as the group average forecasts. The errors of the former were compared with the errors of the latter in terms of the ratio of root mean square errors, $M_i/M_{gi}$. In this expression, $M_i$ refers to the $i$-th member's forecast, and $M_{gi}$ to the corresponding group mean forecast computed as an average of all the individual forecasts that covered the same periods as those included in $M_i$. Only those who had made forecasts on at least five occasions in 1955–62 were included. (Altogether, forecasts were collected semiannually at sixteen dates during that period, each time for six and twelve months ahead.)

Chart 7 shows the distributions of these ratios for the level and change forecasts of GNP, classified by span. The graphs illustrate strikingly the superiority of the group mean forecasts over the individual member forecasts. Only a small part of each of the plotted distributions lies to the left of the line of the unit ratios, in the region where $M_i/M_{gi} < 1$. The distributions are skewed to the right, the best ratios

# CHART 7

*Forty-Seven Individual Forecasts of Levels and Changes of Gross National Product over Spans of Six and Twelve Months (Set D), Comparisons with Mean Forecasts, 1956–63*

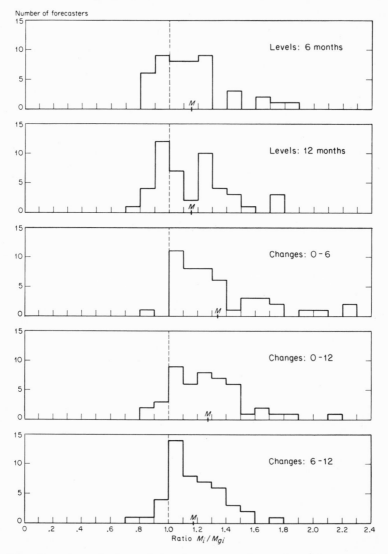

NOTE: In each panel, the vertical scale represents the number of forecasters (members of group D). The horizontal scale represents the ratios of root mean square errors for the individual forecasts and the corresponding group mean forecasts, $M_i/M_{gi}$ (see text for further explanation).

The broken vertical line, drawn through the points of the unit ratios on the horizontal axes, separates the ratios that indicate the superiority of the individual over the mean forecasts (to the left) from the ratios that indicate the opposite (to the right).

The points labeled "$M$" on the horizontal axes locate the mean $M_i/M_{gi}$ ratio in each case.

falling in the classes between 0.7 and 0.9, the worst ones in those between 1.6 and 2.2. The means of the ratios are identified on the horizontal axes; they vary from 1.14 to 1.37. The results for the level forecasts show that only fifteen or seventeen men, out of the forty-seven
included, did better than the group means. For change forecasts, the
proportions are still smaller (one to six of the forty-seven members,
depending on the span).

It should be clear that all this applies strictly to the summary
measures of error over time. In any particular period, many forecasters
(probably about half of them) would produce more accurate forecasts
than the group mean, but very few do so *consistently*. In fact, those
who "beat" the mean forecast for the six-month span are not necessarily the same as those who did so for the twelve-month span (only ten
out of the eighteen forecasters with ratios of less than one for either
span had ratios of less than one for both spans).

The reason for the superiority of the average forecast is that it
is helped by the cancellation of individual errors of opposite sign. It
is easy to see that, unless all the errors (for all forecasters in the group
and for each period covered) have the same sign, the absolute mean of
the errors of the average forecast will be less than the absolute mean
of all the individual forecast errors. (In the special—and unlikely—
case where all errors have the same sign, the two means will be equal.)
This must be so simply because the absolute value of a sum is smaller
than (or at most equal to) the sum of absolute values. A similar argument applies to variances and therefore also to the mean square error
measures.

The forecasters who did better than the group mean not only underestimated GNP less than others but also were more consistent in the
sense of having smaller error variances, as required by the above rea-
soning. A few performed about as well as the best of the forecasts reviewed in the earlier parts of this report, which indicates the high degree of dispersion that may often be concealed by averages for large
groups of forecasters. The accompanying tabulation may serve as an
illustration, although the comparisons it provides are inevitably
crude: [2]

[2] The numbers of observations per span are as follows: Forecaster one-14; two-
15; three-7; mean forecast, group D-16. To compare the results for other forecast
sets, see Table 18.

| | Six-Month Level Forecasts | | Twelve-Month Level Forecasts | |
|---|---|---|---|---|
| | $R_1$ | $R_2{}^*$ | $R_1$ | $R_2{}^*$ |
| Forecaster one, set D | .515 | .900 | .407 | .924 |
| Forecaster two, set D | .456 | .821 | .498 | 1.095 |
| Forecaster three, set D | .421 | .775 | .475 | .860 |
| Mean group forecast D | .549 | .983 | .527 | 1.136 |

As suggested by Chart 7 and the $R$ ratios for the mean forecast D, most of the individual forecasts in set D were able to pass the test of N1 but not that of N2*. Computations matching strictly the periods covered by each forecast confirm this inference. Similar results have been obtained for the forecasts of industrial production made by the individual members of group D.

### RANKING THE FORECAST SETS

Definite conclusions on the relative performance of different forecasters presuppose a comparability that is seldom found in practice. Some variables are more difficult to predict than others and some periods present greater difficulties than others; hence, strict comparability would require forecasts for the same variable and for the same period. Late forecasts can take advantage of recent information not available for earlier forecasts: hence, the predictions, to be comparable, should also be issued at about the same dates. And there are still other factors that affect the answer to the seemingly simple and always intriguing question "Who forecasts best?"

It is not part of the purpose of this study to determine who the best forecasters are. Nevertheless, the question is inevitably asked and cannot well be ignored. Answering it with fairness is usually difficult and may even often prove impossible, but the process of finding this out can itself be instructive. It is in this spirit that some comparisons are made here between forecasts from different sources. The latter are not identified and this exercise is intended to be primarily of analytical interest.

The first step was to rank the sets of annual forecasts of GNP according to their root mean square errors $(M)$, using the maximum number of comparisons that could be made over identical periods of time. Difficulties are at once encountered, since the rankings are not the same in the different periods covered, and the period common to all the forecasts is short. However, the rankings do show some consistency, at least at the extremes. Thus, sets G and F, which cover all the years of comparisons (1953–63), have the lowest $M$ values in all subperiods in which they were matched with the other forecasts.[3] Set E has the lowest rank in each case, and set D the second lowest on most occasions. The range of these summary error measures is very large, e.g., in 1953–63, the smallest $M$ equalled \$8.2 billion and the largest \$17.2 billion.

The intermediate ranks (3 to 6) are occupied by sets B, A, H, and C. Here there is little consistency, e.g., set A ranks lower than set B in 1954–63 but higher in 1956–63 and 1958–63. Some of the observed differences between the $M$ values that underlie these ranks are small and may not be significant.

The ranks for the errors of level and change forecasts show substantial correlation (Spearman's correlation coefficient for the average ranks is .88). But there are some apparently systematic differences, notably set F is better than set G for changes, while the reverse is true for the levels.

Ranking the forecasts according to any of the $M$-ratios based on the extrapolative benchmark models ($R_1$, $R_2$, etc.) must, of course, yield the same results as ranking according to the $M_P$ values proper, if the periods covered are the same.[4] If the assumption that an extrapolative model provides equally good predictions of a given variable in different periods were warranted, the use of the model should enable one to make fair comparisons between forecasts of that variable made by different persons for different time periods. Unfortunately, the assumption is not a safe one. An extrapolative technique may work significantly better in some periods than in others because of differences in the behavior of the given series in the time intervals concerned. Some such differences exist even among the periods covered by our present

---

[3] All eight sets were ranked for 1958–63, all but one (C) for 1956–63, and all but two (C and D) for 1954–63. Rankings of the sets G, F, B, and E were also obtained for 1953–63. See Table 16 for the longest periods used in these computations and the corresponding $M$ values.

[4] The ratios $M_P/M_N$ have a common denominator for all the forecasts in a given period (it is a certain specific value of $M_{N1}$ for the ratios $R_1$, of $M_{N2}$ for the ratios $R_2$, etc.). A given extrapolative model provides a specific standard of performance with which to compare the various forecasts proper; such a standard is clearly not needed to appraise the performance of the forecasts relative to each other, where they all refer to the same series.

investigation, though they all relate to one short phase of recent economic history and partially overlap.

The individual company forecasts (G, F, B) come out well in the comparisons for GNP. The large group forecasts D and E trail, despite the advantages of aggregation described in the previous section. (But a few members of group D did about as well as the best item on our list, and the same may apply to group E, though it could not be tested for lack of individual data.) It is tempting to infer that predictions made by individuals or small teams are, in general, better than those by a large group of forecasters. Rationalizations for such an inference are easy to find. First, the errors of an individual are visible, at least potentially, since his forecast is issued separately; whereas those of a group are not, or hardly at all, since the forecast is submerged in an anonymous poll. As a result, individual forecasts are likely to be more disciplined than those contributed to a poll. Second, some participants in group forecasting, particularly in large polls, may simply be expressing relatively uninformed opinions or guesses; the average level of competence in a large group may be quite low.[5]

Comparisons of industrial production forecasts are inconclusive because the summary measures of error show small differences. Thus the six $M$ values for 1954–63 fall into the range of 4.9 to 6.0 index points; six of the seven for 1958–63, in the range of 5.1 to 5.9. Also, there is still less rank consistency here than in the case of GNP. However, the large-poll median forecast E again ranks last in 1958–63 and next to last in 1954–63. Forecast D, produced by a smaller and more select group, is also relatively weak (it ranks fourth in 1954–63 and sixth, i.e., next to last, in 1958–63). All this is at least not inconsistent with the preceding argument.

There is one mitigating factor, however, in the case against these group forecasts—one that qualifies all the above comparisons—and this is the time when the forecasts are made. In our collection of year-end forecasts, D, E, and B were made in October; A and (sometimes) C in November–December; F, G, and often C in January; and H includes predictions issued at various dates scattered between October and January.

---

[5] This position was taken by Gordon McKinley in his discussion of my preliminary report on the NBER forecasting study at the 1964 Annual Meeting of the American Statistical Association in Chicago.

Since 1950, the first estimates of GNP for a given quarter are provided by the Council of Economic Advisers one month after the close of the quarter. Thus, early in October all that a forecaster may know is the latest GNP figure recorded for the second quarter; in November or December, his knowledge is likely to extend to the estimate for the third quarter; and late in January he may have the first CEA estimates for the fourth quarter. Not only that, but other important data that are demonstrably helpful in forecasting, such as the McGraw-Hill Survey of Investment Intentions, are not available before November.[6] It is clear, therefore, that the relative earliness of sets D and E and the associated deficit of informational inputs may have much to do with the low ranks of these forecasts; though there is reason to believe that this is not the entire explanation and that the other explanations advanced above may still be valid.[7]

Also, for industrial production forecasts lateness is probably of considerably less help than for GNP forecasts, since the production data are available monthly. (The reduced importance of the variation in forecast dates may be one reason why the $M$ values differ so much less for industrial production than for GNP.) But here, too, the ranks of sets D and E are low, while those of sets F and G are high.

In addition to their late timing, the GNP forecasts in set G have one advantage of a special kind. They were given originally in base-year prices (with several shifts of the base). For comparisons with other forecasts, we had to convert them to current dollars; but in so doing we imputed perfect price predictions. This is probably responsible in some part for the high rank of G, since the other forecasts (made in current dollars) undoubtedly include a component of error due to imperfect price predictions.[8]

[6] On the predictive value of investment anticipations, see above pp. 96 to 97.

[7] Thus, for GNP, forecasts D and E are also markedly inferior to B, which was also quite early. (It was usually sent to the printer during the last week of October.)

[8] It should be noted that set G has lower $R$ ratios (i.e., comes out better relative to the benchmark models) when both forecasts and extrapolations are expressed in current dollars than when both are given in the base-year prices, though the differences are not large. This is consistent with the argument in the text.

However, errors of price-change predictions could conceivably be such as to reduce, rather than add to, the total errors. This would be so in the case of offsetting errors, when, e.g., the price-change errors were positive and the errors in predicting the change in constant dollar values were negative. This shows that the situation envisaged in the text, where the advantage is on the side of the constant dollar forecasts, need not always apply, though it is presumably more likely than others.

It should be clear by now that, because of their typical diversity in several aspects, it is extremely difficult to give the forecasts any meaningful over-all grades. Yet the catalogue of problems is still longer. Our evidence, although wide as forecast studies go, covers short periods; hence the samples are still small. To extend the evidence, it is desirable to add the comparisons of chain forecasts to those of annual forecasts, but this entails further complications. The multiperiod forecasts are even less comparable than the annual ones, since they are issued at different times and with different frequencies. Only partial adjustments for these divergencies can be made, and they considerably reduce the number of observations available for these comparisons. Finally, the results based on chain forecasts do not necessarily agree with those obtained for the annual data.[9] One probable source of such differences lies in the role of turning-point errors, which is greater for the chain forecasts than for the annual forecasts. It is not difficult to see that the turning-point criterion may yield different results from the average-errors criterion. While the latter has the advantage of using more information, the former places a greater premium on genuine contributions of forecasters as distinguished from mere extrapolative techniques. Efficient trend projections can produce relatively small average errors for series such as GNP, but not a good turning-point record.

Moreover, differences among averages that cover periods of several years have little meaning if the variation of the underlying values from year to year is very great. It is, therefore, desirable to examine the relative positions of forecasters according to accuracy in each successive year. This will be done presently with a view to establishing how stable or variable these positions are.

### CONSISTENCY OF FORECASTERS' PERFORMANCE

A measure of the degree of over-all agreement among several rankings is provided by the coefficient of concordance $W$. In the case of perfect consistency, each forecast set would preserve the same rank throughout, which yields $W = 1$. In the case of least (zero) consistency, the sum of ranks earned in all periods covered would be the same for each forecast set, namely, equal to the mean value of such sums; here the rankings

[9] For example, the former are much less favorable to set G than the latter are, as suggested by Tables 16 and 18.

are random or uncorrelated, and $W = 0$. The coefficient of concordance is closely associated with the average of all the rank correlation coefficients that can be computed from the same ordered data.[10]

In Table 1, six forecast sets (all except C and D) cover the ten years 1954–63; we can, therefore, construct for them ten rankings according to the absolute values of their errors in each year as listed therein. For these data, the value of $W$ is 0.123 and the average rank correlation coefficient is 0.138. According to an approximate test based on Fisher's Z-distribution, these values are not significant at the 5 per cent level.[11] Even lower $W$ coefficients were obtained for another combination of forecasts and periods ($W = .076$ for the eight forecast sets in 1958–63). And the results for industrial production point in the same direction; here $W = .031$ for six sets of predictions of annual changes for 1954–63.

When the individual ranks for each set are averaged over the years 1954–63, the results do agree broadly with the rankings according to the $M_P$ values, which were discussed in the preceding section: for example, the individual company forecasts are again found at the top of the list for GNP. But it is clear that the averages conceal a great deal of variation in the ranks: the relative positions of the forecasters according to accuracy show many shifts from one year to another. This puts in doubt the evidence of the averages. The less stable the individual ranks, the less meaningful it is to compare the average ranks; and if the former show no significant consistency, then the significance of differences among the latter is also questionable.

The heterogeneity of the forecast sets with respect to the degree of aggregation and dates of issue is troublesome in this context as in others. Some work has been done with the individual forecasts by

---

[10] Let $m$ be the number of rankings and $n$ that of items that are being ranked (in the present case, $m$ would be the number of periods and $n$ the number of forecast sets). The grand total of ranks, divided by $n$, gives the mean value of the sum of ranks per item, $\frac{1}{2} m (n + 1)$. Let $S$ be the sum of squared deviations of the observed sums of ranks from that mean value. Then $W = \dfrac{12S}{m^2(n^3 - n)}$. The mean of the corresponding rank correlation coefficients (Spearman) can be written as $\dfrac{mW - 1}{m - 1}$. On the theory underlying the measurement of concordance, see Maurice G. Kendall, *Rank Correlation Methods*, London, 1948, Chapter 6.

[11] This is based on a table given in Milton Friedman, "A Comparison of Alternative Tests of Significance for the Problem of $m$ Rankings," *Annuals of Mathematical Statistics*, March 1940, pp. 86 ff. (reprinted in Kendall, *Rank Correlation Methods*, Appendix Table 6).

members of group D, which has the advantage of avoiding these problems. For GNP, nine members made forecasts on all occasions, that is, sixteen times at regular semiannual intervals in 1955–62. An analysis of the ranks of their twelve-month forecasts yields $W = 0.111$. This again is not significant at the 5 per cent level. For industrial production, ten members have made forecasts on all occasions in 1958–62, that is, nine times at semiannual intervals. In this case, the coefficient $W$ for twelve-month forecasts is 0.106, which is likewise not significant at the conventional levels.[12]

According to the concordance analysis, then, the variation among the ranks of errors appears to be governed largely by chance. Nevertheless, an inspection of the ranks suggests that some of their shifts can be related to such "systematic" factors as the forecaster's bias and the variation in size of the observed changes in the predicted series. Thus one of the forecast sets ranked first (had the smallest errors) in years of high rates of economic growth—1955, 1959, and 1963—but ranked last in years in which the advance slackened—1960 and 1962. This can be linked with the fact that this forecast set exhibited a strong tendency to overestimate GNP increases in recent years (see Table 2, line 9). On the other hand, one of the sets that had a strong underestimation bias ranked at or near the bottom in most years but was first in 1954, 1960, and 1962, years that witnessed recessions or temporary slowdowns in growth (see line 7 in Tables 1 and 2).

### SIZE OF PREDICTED CHANGES AND FORECASTING ERRORS

The next step, prompted by the above observations, was to rank the forecasters according to the absolute size of the changes they predicted for each period and to apply concordance analysis to these ranks. The forecasts covered are the same as those in the preceding analysis of the ranks of errors.

The coefficients of concordance $W$ are in each case much larger for the ranks of predicted changes than for those of errors. For the six sets of GNP forecasts covering the years 1954–63, $W = 0.403$; for the

[12] The table mentioned in footnote 11 is limited to certain low values of $m$ and $n$. For larger values, the $F$-test may be used, where $F = \dfrac{(m-1)\,W}{1-W}$ with degrees of freedom $n_1 = n - 1 - \dfrac{2}{m}$ and $n_2 = (m-1)\,n_1$. See Helen M. Walker and Joseph Lev, *Statistical Inference*, New York, 1953, p. 285.

TABLE 23

*Relation Between Predicted Changes and Errors:*

*Selected Individual Forecasters of GNP*

*(1955-63) and Industrial Production (1958-63)*

| Forecast Period[a] | Gross National Product | | Industrial Production | |
|---|---|---|---|---|
| | $\rho$[b] | Recorded Change[c] | $\rho$[b] | Recorded Change[d] |
| 6/55- 6/56 | −0.73 | 23.4 | | |
| 12/55-12/56 | −0.63 | 19.4 | | |
| 6/56- 6/57 | −0.88 | 23.7 | | |
| 12/56-12/57 | −0.15 | 14.9 | | |
| 6/57- 6/58[e] | +1.00 | −11.4 | | |
| 12/57-12/58[e] | +0.63 | 4.2 | | |
| 6/58- 6/59 | −0.97 | 44.6 | | |
| 10/58-10/59 | 0 | 30.4 | −0.52 | 12.00 |
| 3/59- 3/60 | +0.35 | 22.7 | −0.43 | 8.00 |
| 10/59-10/60[e] | +1.00 | 19.6 | +0.99 | 2.00 |
| 3/60- 3/61[e] | +1.00 | 4.4 | +0.87 | −1.98 |
| 10/60-10/61 | −0.39 | 29.2 | −0.29 | 13.72 |
| 4/61- 4/62 | −0.70 | 41.5 | +0.60 | 15.24 |
| 10/61-10/62[f] | +0.48 | 29.0 | +1.00 | 7.62 |
| 4/62- 4/63[f] | −0.95 | 27.3 | −0.86 | 8.38 |
| 10/62-10/63 | −0.88 | 33.4 | +0.22 | 10.97 |

Source: Forecasts of nine individual members of group D for GNP and forecasts of ten individual members of group D for industrial production (see text).

[a]The span of each forecast is twelve months. The first date shows when forecasts were made.

[b]Correlation between ranks based on absolute values of predicted changes and ranks based on absolute values of errors (see text).

[c]Early estimate of the actual change in GNP in billion dollars.

[d]Early estimate of the actual change in industrial production in index points, 1947-49 = 100.

[e]These periods include several months of business recession.

[f]These periods include a few months of business retardation in the second half of 1962.

eight sets that are available for 1955–63, $W = 0.442$. The six sets of industrial production forecasts relating to 1954–63 yield $W = 0.433$. All these coefficients are significant at the 1 per cent level.[13]

The data for the individual forecasters in group D produce the following values of $W$: for GNP, 0.383; for industrial production, 0.200. The former figure is highly significant at the 1 per cent level, the latter is just significant at the 5 per cent level.

Forecasters who predicted relatively large changes in most years, as indicated by the averages of these ranks, were more accurate than those who predicted small changes. The average ranks based on the size of anticipated changes show significant negative correlations with the ranks determined according to the over-all errors ($M$) of the same forecast sets. As the values were all ordered in the same direction (from the lowest to the highest), a negative coefficient means that forecasts of relatively small changes were associated, on the average, with relatively large errors. For the six sets of GNP forecasts, 1954–63, the Spearman rank correlation coefficient (adjusted for ties) is $-0.657$; for the industrial production forecasts in the same period, it is $-0.486$.

However, in times of declines or slowdowns in economic activity, the "timid" forecasters who predicted relatively small changes would come out ahead of those who foresaw larger changes (typically, increases). In such periods, therefore, the correlations between the predicted changes and the errors are likely to be positive. For the individual forecasters in group D, rank correlations between changes and errors were computed for each of the overlapping twelve-month periods covered (Table 23). It will be noted that the positive correlations are indeed, with few exceptions, related to periods of business contraction or retardation.

[13] This is strongly indicated by the $F$-tests defined in footnote 12. (Corrections for continuity have been applied, without affecting the results materially.)

# 8

# RELATED STUDIES AND PLANS

THIS is a progress report on one part of the National Bureau study of short-term economic forecasting. It should be useful to give some indications about the work being done in other related areas of the project.

While the present analysis deals with forecasts made without a formal specification of the underlying model or method, another paper in progress covers forecasts which have an explicit basis in econometric models, i.e., in sets of mathematical equations designed to represent the interrelations among economic variables operating over time. Both studies are concerned mainly with accuracy of numerical forecasts. Preliminary results obtained by Jon Cunnyngham suggest that econometric models have been on the average about as accurate as the better general business forecasts in predicting the annual changes of GNP during the period 1953–63.[1]

Rendigs Fels has examined reports on the business outlook in a collection of influential business and financial periodicals with a view to evaluating their record on the recognition of cyclical turning points. He finds that warnings that proved right come typically late and that false signals have been frequent on some occasions. To recognize contemporaneously a peak or a trough (that is, to predict turning points with a zero lead) would be to perform better than the average of the publications reviewed.[2] This is consistent with our finding that "the record of the numerical forecasts of GNP . . . does not indicate an ability to forecast the turn several months ahead."

[1] See Forty-Fifth Annual Report, New York, National Bureau of Economic Research, 1965, p. 60. The econometric models are expressed in terms of changes in constant dollars and the comparisons assume error-free price predictions in all forecasts involved.

[2] *Ibid.*, p. 64.

Jacob Mincer and myself have worked on the methodology of forecast evaluation with the aim of formulating and applying in an ex-
ploratory manner some criteria for analyzing aspects of predictive per-
formances.[3] The approach developed in this study is also used in other
parts of our project which are concerned with the quality of numerical
forecasts. Some of the results are seen as pertinent to the general subject of economics of expectations, beyond the narrower question of
how to appraise forecasting accuracy.

Errors in the data used by the forecaster account for nearly all of
the error in the forecast base, according to Rosanne Cole's study of
GNP revisions and their relation to forecasting accuracy. Predictions of
changes are affected significantly by such errors in those cases where
projection of past values of the series is an important ingredient of the
forecast. For some of the forecast sets covered by the present report,
very little of the error in predicted change could be traced to errors
in the GNP figures as estimated from data revisions; for other sets, it
appears that as much as 20 per cent of the error in change forecasts
was induced by the thus measured errors of observation.[4]

Less closely related to this study is the research conducted by Geoffrey H. Moore and Julius Shiskin, which is concerned with improvement of forecasting tools rather than with evaluation of any recorded
forecasts. Moore and Shiskin have completed a comprehensive review
of the National Bureau cyclical indicators and compiled a revised list
based on several objective criteria and an explicit and inclusive scor-
ing system. The result should be a better selection, classification, and
description of business cycle indicators.

### FURTHER RESEARCH

An inventory of findings usually reveals gaps to be filled as well as
doubts to be resolved. Some observations are, therefore, in order about
a few other topics that either are under study or deserve future attention.

The comparative merits and shortcomings of different forecasting
methods and procedures are, of course, matters of central interest, but

[3] Forty-Sixth Annual Report, New York, National Bureau of Economic Research,
1966, pp. 53–54.

[4] See also the reports by Rosanne Cole in the National Bureau Annual Reports for
1965 and 1966.

direct information on the methods used is largely lacking and would be difficult and costly to collect. Most forecasters use various techniques (extrapolations, relationships among economic variables, business surveys) in combination, tempering the results by judgment. They themselves may not be able, therefore, to determine retrospectively the precise relative importance of these ingredients. A more promising approach to the problem of evaluating forecasting methods is an indirect one, based on comparisons of summary error measures for different types of predictions of the same variable. Some of the following suggestions for research illustrate possible applications of this approach.

1. Comparisons of actual forecasts with various types of extrapolations, such as those introduced in Chapter 6 of the present study, can be extended to provide relative measures of predictive accuracy which distinguish between the systematic (bias) and the random parts of the errors. This analysis also results in estimates of the "autonomous" and "extrapolative" components of forecasts, or how much forecasts and extrapolations have in common and how large are the net predictive contributions of each. The methodology for these measurements has already been developed (see Chapter 6, note 2).

2. Comparisons could be made between econometric model forecasts and more informal forecasts, and between the recorded forecasts and predictions that could be obtained from anticipations data and leading indicators. This work would also produce measures of relative over-all accuracy, bias, and efficiency, formally analogous to those generated by comparisons of forecasts with extrapolations. Some tentative results on econometric model forecasts have already been obtained, as noted before. The sum of these efforts should result in some tested quantitative estimates of the contributions to effective forecasting of techniques such as econometric relations, anticipations and indicator data, extrapolation procedures, and (as a residual) "judgment."

3. Analysis of the structure of forecasts from a given source, that is, relations between the predicted values of such elements of the economic system as aggregate income, consumption, investment, government expenditures, etc., would be useful. For example, one may ask what "consumption function" is implied in a forecast, or, specifically, what the coefficients of a regression of predicted consumption on predicted income are. These relations would then be compared with their counterparts for the actual values. Such analysis can provide important

clues on how a forecast was constructed in those cases where the fore-caster's model is not specified (and this category includes the majority of all business conditions forecasts).

4. Appraisals of the general business outlook nowadays most often take the form of forecasts of the size and structure of GNP *in current dollars*. On the other hand, economic theory suggests that some rela-tions of concern to the forecaster apply to quantities or constant-dollar values, and the latter are used by some forecasters, notably those working with econometric models. It is of considerable interest to examine two questions: How accurate have the price forecasts been? How did the errors of these forecasts affect the forecasts of GNP? Pre-liminary results indicate that price level predictions in recent years have been on the whole unsatisfactory. Price changes were often understated when they were large and overstated when they were small. However, the effects of the price errors on the GNP forecasts have not always been adverse because of elements of negative correlation between these errors and those in the implicit quantity component of GNP.

5. Aggregation of forecasts may obscure some interesting aspects of forecasting. Additional materials now available represent a substantial extension of our collection of individual forecasts and will permit us to study the latter more intensively. It will be possible to examine the distributions of predicted changes and compare them with those of actual changes for several different variables and subperiods. Evidence on how the errors of individuals are structured and how they are asso-ciated with each other at different times will be considerably increased, which may improve understanding of how forecasts are formed and how forecasters interact.

6. Further insights into how to improve the use of available infor-mation for purposes of forecasting can be gained from assessments of the quality of forecast revisions. Our compilation contains materials that are uniquely suited for such an investigation, namely, forecasts for overlapping sequences of short periods (e.g., predictions for each of several quarters ahead, revised and extended quarterly). Do revisions improve the forecasts significantly and systematically? If improvements are achieved, as seems to be the case, how are they related to the char-acteristics of the forecasts, of the series being predicted, of the period covered? These questions illustrate what we expect to learn from this

part of the study. More ambitiously, we might be able to formulate a useful "learning function"—one that would enable forecasters to learn efficiently from their past errors and that may therefore be expected to help forecasters in the future.

7. The availability and quality of data needed by forecasters are important subjects for study. As already noted, a paper on revisions in the GNP accounts is concerned with some major questions in this field. How large are the errors of observation relative to the errors of forecasts for the same series? Do the revisions of the data reveal systematic measurement errors? If so, are the latter related to the systematic components of forecast errors? Further work in this general area should progress from an analysis of data quality to that of data requirements. Series with anticipatory properties, such as the leading cyclical indicators, the indexes based on surveys of businessmen's plans and consumer intentions, government budget projections, and the so-called diffusion data are of special interest here. Past efforts on this front were rewarded by some significant extensions and improvements in statistical materials. These may prove to be one way of getting better forecasts, and further explorations of this subject are planned.

# INDEX

(Figures in **boldface** type refer to tables and charts)